The Birth of the Augmented Human

The Freeing of Humanity

Richard Lowe

The Writing King

Enemies of You Series

The Birth of the Augmented Human

Table of Contents

See books by Richard Lowe at

https://masterofworlds.com

5

Get free publishing insights and industry updates at

https://thewritingking.substack.com

For ghostwriting and book coaching services see

https://thewritingking.com

Enemies of You Series

https://masterofworlds.com/enemies-of-you

The Death of Thinking

The Enslavement of Humanity

The Birth of the Augmented Human

The Freeing of Humanity

Turn Off The TV, Get Off Your Ass, and Do Something

Stuck in the Middle

Wars, Weapons, and the Forces That Will Shape the Next Thirty Years

The Enshittification of America

How Private Equity Destroyed the Things We Love

The Emasculation of America

How Russia's Long War Against the American Male Is Destroying the Nation From Within

The Villainization of America

———

See the full series description at the back of this book.

All books available at masterofworlds.com

Preface

The companion volume, The Death of Thinking: The Enslavement of Humanity, ended with a question. This book is the answer, which is also the beginning of another question, which is how honest answers usually work.

This book is the third in a series. Turn Off the TV, Get Off Your Ass, and Do Something addressed passive consumption: the life going unlived while the feeds refreshed. The Death of Thinking addressed cognitive dependency: the thinking going undone while the AI drafted. This book addresses the alternative: the practitioner who maintains their own cognitive engagement with the tools available to them, and what that maintenance produces over time. The trilogy moves from the couch to the prompt to the practice. This is the third step.

The Death of Thinking mapped the problem. It found the problem in the specific practitioners it followed, Ray, Sasha, Donna, Tom, Elena, Deon, Priya, Nina, Fatima, James, Gideon, Laura, and in the structural forces that produced the problem and are accelerating it. The commercial design of AI tools. The education system that met AI halfway. The governance gap. The slow democratic deficit. The five civilizational threats that cognitive erosion makes harder to address. The diagnosis was accurate and is not reassuring.

This book does not contradict that diagnosis. The trajectory described in the companion volume is real. The structural forces are real. The cognitive erosion is real and appears to be accumulating. What this book argues is that within that trajectory, on that terrain, a different outcome is available. Not for everyone. Not without cost. For practitioners who understand what the cost is and what they are buying with it.

The augmented human is that outcome. Not a theory, not a prediction about what the technology will eventually make possible. A specific kind of practitioner, identifiable by specific practices, producing specific results that the current dominant path cannot produce. The augmented human is real and is already working, in the specific people this book follows on the other path, whose work is the evidence for the claim this book makes.

The claim is not optimistic in the way popular books about AI tend to be optimistic. It does not argue that everything will be fine, that the market will eventually reward cognitive development over cognitive dependency, that the education system will reform itself in time, that the structural forces the companion volume described will reverse on a schedule that protects the generation currently developing. None of that is true. The claim is narrower and more defensible: the other path is available to people who pursue it, it produces something real, and the production is worth the cost.

The practices described in this book are what the other path consists of. They are not difficult to understand. They are against the grain of every commercial incentive in the current AI environment, which is why most practitioners are not maintaining them and why the practitioners who are produce something different. What differs is the subject of this book.

One note on structure: this book is shorter than its companion because prescriptions should be more concise than diagnoses. The problem required twenty-one chapters to establish with the specificity that makes it credible and practical. The other path requires twenty-one chapters to describe with the specificity that makes it buildable. But the chapters are shorter, because the other path does not require as much explanation as the current one does. The current path is complex in its causes and ramifying in its consequences. The other path is simple in its principle and requires mostly the will to maintain it.

Introduction: The Other Path Does Not Announce Itself

I wrote this book because AI, when used correctly, is a force multiplier of value that has no real precedent. Not a replacement for thinking, but an amplifier of it. You can increase your productivity, improve the quality of your decisions, build better relationships because you are better informed, and become genuinely more capable across almost every domain of your life. That is not hype. It is what I have seen happen when people engage with these tools the right way instead of outsourcing their thinking to them. The companion book documents what goes wrong when people do the latter. This book is about what goes right when they do the former.

The other path does not announce itself. It does not come with a credential or a certification or a professional title. It does not show up in productivity metrics, at least not in the early stages, and it is not rewarded by most of the environments where most practitioners work. It shows up in the work, eventually, in the ways that matter most: in the quality of judgment under pressure, in the distinctiveness of perspective, in the capacity to produce something genuine when the assignment is genuinely hard.

This book is about what produces that capacity. Specifically: the practices that maintain and develop the human cognitive functions that AI tools are designed, by commercial necessity, to replace. The practices are not dramatic. They are a notebook before the AI is opened. A paragraph written before the structure is requested. A hypothesis formed before the diagnostic tool is consulted. A position stated before the framing is provided. Small choices in sequence that accumulate, over months and years, into a practitioner who is genuinely more capable, more original, more diagnostic, more able to surprise themselves, than the practitioner who did not make them.

The companion volume described what the absence of these practices produces. This book describes what their presence produces.

Part One, The Other Path, follows the book's characters on the path not taken in the companion volume. Ray writing his paragraph before the AI sees the assignment. Sasha sitting with the logs before consulting the diagnostic tool. Donna in the swamp, treating the discomfort as productive rather than as a problem to be solved. Tom building the argument sketch before the AI provides the structure. Priya writing the prior statement before the research begins. These are not triumphant stories. The other path is not a path where things go obviously better or where the environment rewards the choices being made. It is a path where something is being built that the environment cannot yet see.

Part Two, How It Gets Built, examines the conditions that produce augmentation. The long development arc that the other path requires. The design principles that would make development rather than dependency the default outcome of AI tools, and why those principles are commercially disadvantaged against the current design. What teaching thinking looks like in classrooms, households, and mentoring relationships where individual choice can still determine what develops. The governance question from the inside: what the augmented practitioner can do within the structural environment described in the companion volume.

Part Three, What It Makes Possible, describes what the other path produces at scale: the individual augmented, the generation at the fork, the professions that maintain their development pipeline, the democracy with the epistemic infrastructure that democratic deliberation requires, the culture of inquiry, the existential stakes and the individual contribution to addressing them.

Part Four, The Architecture, is about what would need to change for the other path to be available to more than the minority who currently seek it out. What AI tools designed for development rather than dependency would look like. What the new literacy means and how it is taught. What the specific design properties are that the augmented practitioner can demand from the tools they use. What a policy framework for human augmentation looks like and what its minimum viable interventions are.

The book ends where the companion volume ended: with an answer that opens back into a question. The augmented human is the answer to what you are building, if you are building it. What you do with that answer, whether you pursue the other path, whether you maintain it when the environment works against it, whether you contribute to making it available to more people, is still your question.

The companion volume gave you the question. This book gives you the other path. The path is open. Here is the map.

Part One: The Other Path

Chapter One: The Question Worth Asking

The other book in this pair ended with a question. This one is the answer , or the beginning of one, which is as much as any book can honestly claim to be.

The question was: what are you building? The answer this book is interested in is not the one about outputs. It is not the productivity numbers, the content volume, the deployment velocity, the quarterly earnings that follow from AI integration at scale. Those answers exist and are easy to find and are not what this book is for.

The answer this book is interested in is the one about the person. What kind of person are you building, through the choices you make about how you use the tools available to you. Whether the compound return on those choices, accumulated over years, produces a practitioner who is genuinely more capable, more original, more diagnostic, more surprising to themselves, or a practitioner who is faster and less of those things. Both outcomes are available. Both are already happening. This book is about the one that is harder to see because it does not show up in any productivity metric and does not announce itself in any quarterly report.

Ray is in it, on the other path, in the version of his story where he took it. So is Sasha. So are Gideon and Fatima and Priya. None of their stories are triumphant in the way that is easy to write. The other path is not a path where things go obviously better or where the environment rewards the choices being made. It is a path where something is being built that the environment cannot currently see, that the market does not currently price, and that the person on it knows is real because of what happens when the novel situation arrives, when the assignment has no template, when the system fails in a way that has no precedent, when the problem requires the thing that was being quietly built rather than the thing the tools have been supplying.

That moment is the test. This book is about how to pass it.

What the Augmented Human Actually Is

The word augmented has been used in this context to mean two different things, and the difference matters enough to establish at the start.

The first meaning is prosthetic: AI supplements human capability the way a calculator supplements arithmetic, handling a function the person would otherwise have to perform manually. The person remains the same. Their output is faster or more voluminous or more polished. What they can do without the tool is unchanged. This is the version that most AI integration produces, and it is genuinely useful in the domains where the supplemented function was the bottleneck. It is not what this book means by augmentation.

The second meaning is generative: AI interaction actively develops the person's capability over time, so that what the person can do without the tool increases. The tool is being used in a way that produces growth rather than just output. The practitioner who uses AI to challenge their own thinking, to stress-test their own arguments, to surface the failure modes of their own code before those failure modes encounter reality, this practitioner is using AI in a way that makes them better at the underlying work, not just faster at the visible product of it.

The augmented human in the second sense is not a fantasy. They are a specific kind of person, with specific practices, using the same tools that are producing the dependency gradient described in The Death of Thinking. The technology is identical. The outcome is opposite. What differs is entirely in what the person brings to the tool and what they require of themselves before the tool is consulted.

Mamoru Oshii's Ghost in the Shell, which closes the companion volume, ends with a merger. The human ghost intact, the shell extended. The merger produces something neither component could have become alone. This is the image this book is building toward: not the human replaced, not the human diminished, but the human whose own capacity, the ghost, the specific and developed and irreducible part, is genuinely extended by the tools rather than gradually substituted by them.

The path to that merger requires the ghost to be present. Developed, maintained, exercised against resistance. This book is about how that happens.

Ray on the Other Path

In the version of Ray's story where the other path is available, the change that matters most happens in a moment that looks like inefficiency.

He opens a new document. The assignment is a long-form piece on why a mid-size technology company's strategic pivot is going to fail. He has done fifty pieces like this. The AI could produce a structure in thirty seconds that he would recognize as competent, that he would then revise toward something that sounds more like him, that his editor would accept, that would be published and read and forgotten.

Instead he writes a paragraph. His paragraph. Rough, not quite right, missing things he will find later. It takes twenty minutes and produces something that is clearly worse, at this stage, than what the AI would have given him. He knows this. He writes it anyway, because the twenty minutes of struggle is when he finds out what he thinks about the company's situation, and the thing he thinks is the only part of the subsequent piece that the AI cannot supply.

The AI arrives after the paragraph exists. He asks it to generate the strongest possible argument that the company's pivot will succeed. Not to write his piece. To attack his position. The AI produces three arguments. Two of them he has already considered and dismissed. The third is one he has not thought of, and it is good, and engaging with it genuinely changes the piece he writes. Not by refuting his thesis, his thesis holds, but by forcing him to account for the strongest version of the opposing case, which makes his own case sharper.

This is the working model. It takes longer than prompting first. It produces better work. Over a year of doing it this way, Ray has developed something that is not visible in any individual piece and is visible in the aggregate: a relationship to his own thinking that is more confident, more specific, more willing to take a position that is genuinely his rather than the AI's synthesis. The blank page still produces discomfort. The discomfort has become information rather than an obstacle. It tells him what he has not yet figured out, which is the thing worth figuring out.

Ray on the other path is not obviously better than Ray on the current one, measured by any metric his editor or his clients are currently using. He is producing work that is more distinctly his, which is sometimes more valuable and sometimes just different. The compound return on the practice is not visible yet in the way that quarterly productivity metrics are visible. It will be visible the day the assignment arrives that has no template, the piece that requires a perspective rather than a synthesis, the editor who says: I don't want research, I want what you think. That day Ray on the other path has something to say. The other Ray has something to generate.

Sasha on the Other Path

In the version of Sasha's story where the other path is available, the change happens in how he debugs.

A service is misbehaving. The logs show what is happening. He knows, from two years of accepting AI-generated explanations for similar behavior, that the AI will produce a plausible diagnosis in seconds. He has learned, from those same two years, that the plausible diagnosis is sometimes right and sometimes a confident wrong answer that costs him three hours of chasing the wrong thing. He has also learned that when he forms his own hypothesis first, however incomplete, the AI's response is more useful: he can evaluate it against his own model rather than accepting it as the model.

So he sits with the logs for ten minutes. Not because he expects to solve the problem in ten minutes. Because ten minutes of genuine engagement with the failure activates his mental model of the system in a way that cold-consulting the AI does not. By the end of the ten minutes he has a hypothesis. It is wrong in its specifics and right in its direction. The AI's response, when he asks for it, gives him the correct explanation, and because he has a prior model to compare it against, the correction is informative in a way that receiving the explanation cold would not have been. The gap between his hypothesis and the correct answer tells him something about his mental model of the system. That information is available because he attempted the hypothesis. It is not available if he skips it.

Over two years of this practice, Sasha's mental model of the systems he works in has gotten more accurate. Not because AI gave it to him. Because the repeated practice of forming hypotheses, comparing them against AI-assisted diagnoses, and identifying the gaps has been systematically correcting his model. The AI is functioning as a calibration tool rather than a replacement tool. The calibration is building something. He can feel it in the way he thinks about new systems: a structural intuition that was not there two years ago, a sense of where things are likely to fail before the failure occurs, a diagnostic instinct that has been built rather than atrophied.

The interview that Sasha failed in The Death of Thinking, the one where he could not explain why the architecture was built the way it was. Sasha on the other path passes. Not because he is more intelligent. Because the why of his architecture is fully his. He built the mental model before the AI implemented it. The implementation is AI-assisted. The judgment that shaped the implementation is not. When the interviewer asks why, he knows.

What This Book Is Not

This book is not optimistic in the way that popular books about AI tend to be optimistic. It is not arguing that everything will be fine, that the trajectory described in The Death of Thinking will self-correct, that the market will eventually reward cognitive development over cognitive dependency, or that institutions will reform themselves in time to protect the capacities this book is arguing are worth protecting.

The trajectory described in the companion volume is the most plausible reading of the available evidence and is not showing signs of reversing. The structural forces producing AI dependency are commercial, powerful, and self-reinforcing. The educational institutions that should be building the foundation are still oriented away from it. The professional environments that should be maintaining the development pipeline are eliminating it. The market that should be pricing the difference between a practitioner who can think independently and one who cannot is mostly not able to see the difference yet.

This book is arguing that within that environment, on that trajectory, a different outcome is available to people who understand what they are building and make specific choices to build it. That is a narrower claim than the popular books make. It is also a more defensible one.

The augmented human is not the inevitable product of AI technology. They are the product of a specific relationship to that technology, maintained against the grain of most of the incentives in the current environment. That relationship requires understanding, practice, and the willingness to accept a real cost in the short term for a benefit that is deferred and invisible by the metrics most environments currently apply.

This book is for the person who is willing to accept that cost because they understand what the benefit is. It is not for the person looking for a productivity hack or a way to use AI better in the sense of getting more output faster. Those books exist and are useful for what they are. This is not one of them.

What the Author Is Not

The companion volume established, in its account of the author's working model, that this book is itself a product of the augmented practice it is describing. The arguments were developed before the AI was consulted about them. The AI was used adversarially, to generate the strongest counterarguments, to find the logical gaps, to surface the cases that the argument needed to account for. The AI did not form the argument. The author formed the argument, tested it against the AI, revised in response to the testing, and is genuinely the author's in the sense that it came from the author's observation of the world and could not have come from the AI alone.

This is not a confession. It is a demonstration. The working model described in Part Four of The Death of Thinking is the working model that produced this book. If the argument in this book is worth reading, it is partly evidence for the argument in this book. If it is not worth reading, that is also information, but a different kind.

The author is not a technologist or a researcher. The observations in these books come from working at the intersection of AI tools and knowledge work for long enough to see the pattern, and from caring enough about the pattern to try to describe it accurately. The descriptions are not neutral. They are argued. This argument is that the augmented human is real, is specific, is achievable by most people who pursue it seriously, and is worth pursuing. The rest of this book is the case for that argument.

The Map of This Book

Part One describes the augmented practitioner in practice: what they do, what it costs them, what it produces over time. Not an idealized account. The specific, sometimes awkward, economically penalized version that exists in the real world.

Part Two describes how augmentation gets built: the conditions that produce it, the developmental arc it requires, the role of education and environment and deliberate practice in creating the foundation that the tools can extend.

Part Three describes what augmentation makes possible at scale: the augmented individual, the profession that maintains its development pipeline, the democracy with cognitive infrastructure, the culture that can hold complexity because enough of its members can.

Part Four describes the architecture: what would need to be true, institutionally and culturally, for the augmented path to be available to more than the minority who currently seek it out against the grain of their environments.

The companion volume ended with a question. This one ends with an answer that is also, in the way that honest answers usually are, the beginning of another question. That structure is intentional. The augmented human is not a destination. It is a practice. The practice does not end.

Chapter Two: The Productive Friction

Donna is a freelance writer with eight years of experience. The Death of Thinking found her in the swamp: the disorganized, uncomfortable early stage of a piece where the angle has not emerged, the structure does not exist, and the writing is all wrong. She eliminated the swamp by prompting the AI for a structure before the swamp had time to do its work. The structure arrived. The piece moved forward. The piece was competent and empty.

This chapter is about what the swamp was producing before she eliminated it. And why eliminating it was the specific mistake it was.

What the Swamp Actually Is

The swamp is not a failure of the writing process. It is the writing process, in its most productive form, before the product becomes visible.

The discomfort of early-stage work, the period of disorganized notes and failed first sentences and arguments that collapse before they get to the second paragraph, is the period when the writer's genuine relationship to the subject is being established. The subject is resisting. The resistance is information. The resistance tells the writer which approaches don't work, which framings don't hold, which angles are obvious in a way that reveals nothing. A writer who stays with the resistance long enough discovers something the AI cannot supply: the angle that only they would find, because it comes from their specific history with the subject, their specific confusions, their specific sense of what is strange or interesting or wrongly understood about it.

The AI does not resist. It produces a competent structure immediately, which is the problem. The competent structure is built from patterns in training data, from the most common ways this kind of piece has been structured before. It is the average of how the subject has been approached. It does not contain the writer's angle because the writer has not been in the swamp long enough to find their angle. The piece moves forward on a foundation that is not the writer's, and the piece knows it. Editors know it. Readers know it, even if they cannot say why. The piece reads like a competent treatment of a subject rather than a person thinking about a subject, and those are different experiences of different value.

Robert Bjork's research on desirable difficulties, described in the companion volume, documents the general principle: conditions that feel harder during acquisition produce more durable and transferable learning. The swamp is the desirable difficulty of the writing process. The difficulty is not incidental to the development of genuine craft. It is the mechanism of it. Bjork's research is primarily lab-based; the extrapolation to professional craft development over years is plausible and consistent with what experienced practitioners report, but has not been measured at that timescale.

The Angle That Only You Would Find

There is a specific kind of insight that emerges from the swamp that cannot be reached by any other route, and it is worth being precise about what it is and why the route matters.

The AI can synthesize. Given a subject, it can produce a comprehensive account of what is known about that subject, what the main positions are, what the evidence suggests, what the relevant considerations are. This synthesis is genuinely useful for many purposes. It is not the angle. The angle is the writer's specific contribution to the subject: the observation that reframes what the synthesis contains, the question that the synthesis raises but does not ask, the connection between this subject and something else the writer has been thinking about that illuminates both. The angle is where the writer's particular experience of the world intersects with the subject. It cannot be synthesized from training data because it requires a specific mind, with its specific history, to find it.

The angle is also fragile in the early stage. It is present as a felt sense before it can be articulated. A writer who has been in the swamp for an hour has something they are trying to say that they cannot yet say clearly. The AI, consulted at this stage, produces a structure that looks like what they were trying to say, and the resemblance is enough to anchor their thinking to the AI's version rather than their own. The AI replaces the felt sense's structure. The piece proceeds. The original angle is lost because it was never fully formed before the external structure arrived to organize the writer's attention around something else.

Donna, in the version of her story where the other path is available, has learned to treat the swamp as the work rather than as the delay before the work. She keeps a notebook. Not to produce anything publishable. To talk to herself on the page about what she is trying to figure out, what she does not yet understand about the subject, what is wrong with the obvious framings and why she finds them unsatisfying. The notebook is not the draft. It is the space where the angle gets found.

The notebook practice is slow. It produces a lot that is not useful. It produces, reliably, a paragraph every few sessions that contains something she would not have found without it, and that paragraph is the piece. Everything else in the final published work is structure and support. The paragraph is the point, and the point is hers.

Friction as a Design Principle

The insight that the swamp is productive rather than wasteful suggests a design principle for the augmented practitioner's relationship to AI tools: friction by design. Not friction as obstacle, not friction as inefficiency to be eliminated, but friction introduced deliberately at the points in the work where productive difficulty would otherwise be removed.

The design principle is specific. It does not apply equally to all parts of the work. There are tasks in any knowledge work where the productive difficulty is not in the initial generation but in the evaluation and refinement: fact-checking, style editing, formatting, looking up information that the writer already knows how to evaluate. For these tasks, AI assistance that removes friction is pure efficiency gain. The friction was not producing development. Removing it costs nothing important.

The productive friction is in the generative stages: the stage where the angle is being found, the argument is being formed, the structure is being discovered. This is the stage where most writers now introduce AI earliest, because it is the most uncomfortable stage, because the AI is most efficient at resolving the discomfort, and because the resolution looks like progress. It is not progress toward the thing that makes the piece worth writing. It is progress toward a piece that will exist.

The augmented writer has internalized the distinction between the generative stage and the evaluative stage, and applies AI assistance primarily to the second. The first is protected. Not forever, not a permanent commitment to manual drafting in all contexts, but consistently enough that the generative work remains the writer's. The AI arrives after something exists that was made by the writer. It challenges, refines, fact-checks, and stress-tests what the writer made. It does not make it.

The programmer's equivalent is design before generation. Sasha on the other path holds the problem in his head long enough to have a view about the architecture before the AI sees the requirements. The view is imperfect and will be improved. This point is not that his initial design is better than what the AI would produce. This point is that having a design before consulting the AI means he can evaluate the AI's response against his own intended approach, rather than accepting the AI's approach as the approach. The evaluation is the development. The development is the compound return.

The Myth of Wasted Time

The most persistent obstacle to embracing productive friction is the conviction that the time spent in the swamp is wasted. A writer who spends two hours in the notebook before opening a draft has spent two hours producing nothing billable. The programmer who spends a morning thinking through an architecture before writing any code has spent a morning not shipping. The economics are real. The conviction follows logically from how most professional environments measure value, which is by output, not by the development that makes future output better.

The conviction is also wrong, in a way that takes years to become visible.

The IKEA effect, cited in the companion volume, describes the tendency to value things more when you have made them yourself. The cognitive version of this is more consequential than the furniture version: understanding that cost you something to acquire is more durable, more flexible, and more available under pressure than understanding that arrived without cost. A writer who fought through the swamp to find the angle has a relationship to that piece of work that is qualitatively different from the writer who accepted an AI structure. Both writers can describe the argument of the piece. Only one of them has it as a felt possession, available for revision and defense and extension in ways that accepted-structure knowledge is not.

The time in the swamp is not wasted. It is not even primarily about the piece being written. It is training. Every session in the swamp is practice in the specific skill of finding an angle where there is not yet one, of staying with a subject long enough for a genuine observation to emerge. This skill compounds. A writer who has been in the swamp a thousand times has a faster and more reliable angle-finding process than the writer who has been in it a hundred times, not because they spend less time in the swamp but because their tolerance for the discomfort is higher and their pattern recognition for when the angle is about to emerge is better calibrated. The compound return is not visible in any individual piece. It is visible across a career.

Donna at three years into the notebook practice is a different writer from Donna at eight months. What differs is not in her output volume or her publication rate or her word count per hour. It is in the quality and distinctiveness of her angles. Her editors have noticed it, though most of them cannot say specifically what changed. The pieces feel more like they came from someone rather than from a process. That is the compound return. It does not show up until it does, and when it does, it is unmistakable.

Adversarial AI as the Swamp's Partner

There is a specific use of AI that is not the enemy of the swamp but its ally: the adversarial mode.

The adversarial mode asks AI to attack what already exists rather than to produce what does not yet exist. A writer who has been in the swamp and found an angle has something to defend. The AI, asked to generate the strongest argument against that angle, produces challenges that are often better than the challenges the writer would construct alone, because the AI can generate the full space of objections rather than only the ones the writer would think of.

The adversarial session is different from the swamp in its structure but continuous with it in its function. The swamp produces the angle. The adversarial session stress-tests it. Both require the writer to do cognitive work that the AI cannot do for them. The swamp requires finding something genuine. The adversarial session requires defending it, or discovering that it cannot be defended, which is equally useful information.

A writer who ends a swamp session with a rough angle and immediately enters an adversarial session with the AI is using the tools in the sequence that produces development rather than dependency. The tools are not being used to replace the writer's thinking. They are being used to sharpen it. The difference in workflow looks small: prompt for a structure versus draft a paragraph, then prompt for challenges to the paragraph. The difference in outcome, accumulated over years, is the difference between a writer who can produce original analysis and a writer who can produce competent synthesis.

Donna uses the adversarial mode after every notebook session that produces something worth using. She takes the rough paragraph, the one that contains the angle, however clumsily stated, and asks the AI: what is wrong with this argument? Tell me the three strongest reasons this framing fails. The AI produces objections. Some of them she has already considered. Some she has not. The ones she has not considered become the revisions that make the piece stronger. The ones she has considered she can now articulate a defense for, which makes the published piece more confident in its position because the position has been tested.

This is the augmented practitioner's relationship to the tools: not cooperative, not submissive, but adversarial in the specific sense of using the tool as a sparring partner rather than a ghostwriter. The sparring partner makes you better. The ghostwriter makes you faster. Faster is commercially rewarded. Better is what the career is built on.

The Practitioner Who Has Lost the Swamp

The Death of Thinking described what happens when the swamp is eliminated over time. The specific damage is worth revisiting here because understanding what was lost is the beginning of understanding how to rebuild it.

A writer who has not been in the swamp for a year has not been practicing angle-finding. The skill has not been used. It has not developed. It may have atrophied. The test for this is simple and uncomfortable: open a document, pick a subject you know well, write a paragraph that says something specific and is genuinely yours before consulting any external source. The paragraph does not have to be good. It has to be an attempt.

A writer who has not been in the swamp recently will find that the paragraph is harder to produce than they expected. The specific difficulty is not lack of knowledge about the subject. It is the absence of a felt sense of what they want to say about it. The knowledge is there. The angle is not. The angle requires the swamp to produce it, and the swamp has not been visited.

This is recoverable. The swamp is not gone. It is unused. The rehabilitation described in the companion volume is the right model: reintroduce the demand gradually. Not by committing to a year of unassisted drafting before AI is allowed anywhere near the work. By committing to the notebook for thirty minutes before the AI is consulted. By requiring one genuine attempt at an angle before the AI structure is invited. The attempt does not have to produce something good. It has to be genuine, which means the writer has to stay in the uncomfortable period long enough for something to emerge or fail to emerge, and either outcome is information.

The rehabilitation timeline varies by how long the swamp has been avoided and how practiced the writer was before the avoidance began. A writer who had ten years of swamp practice before AI tools became available has something to return to. The muscle memory is there, dormant. It responds to exercise faster than the writer who has never developed it. Donna, with eight years before AI, is in a better position to rehabilitate than a writer who graduated into AI-assisted workflows from the start. Both can rebuild. The starting point differs.

What Productive Friction Produces Over Time

The compound return on maintaining productive friction is specific enough to name, because the specificity changes what recovery looks like and what success looks like.

For writers, the capacities that develop through the swamp practice are: original ideation under constraint, the ability to find an angle on a subject within specific parameters without external scaffolding; structural intuition, the ability to feel when an argument has a center and when it does not, before the argument can be fully articulated; and revision toward strength, the ability to identify what is weakest in a piece and make it stronger rather than making it longer or smoother. These are the capacities that distinguish writers who are considered for the hard assignments from writers who are not, that make editors return rather than just file, that make the career compound rather than plateau.

For programmers, the equivalent capacities are: system-level reasoning, the ability to think about how components will interact before implementing any of them; diagnostic intuition, the felt sense that something is wrong with a system before the evidence makes it explicit; and architectural judgment, the ability to evaluate a design against requirements that have not yet been fully specified. These are the capacities that make senior developers, that make architects, that make the practitioners who are called when the system fails in a way no one has seen before.

Neither list is exotic. Both are descriptions of what experienced practitioners develop through years of work with productive friction built in. The AI environment removes the friction. The capacities do not develop. The practitioners produce acceptable outputs for a long time. The test arrives when the assignment is not acceptable output but something more, and the practitioner who has been building rather than just producing has something to bring to it.

Donna at eight years, on the other path, is the writer whose editor calls when the subject is genuinely hard and the piece needs to be genuinely good. Not the most prolific writer on the masthead. The one with the angle. The one who has been in the swamp enough times to know what finding something real feels like, and who finds it, reliably, because the practice has made it reliable. That is what the productive friction produces. It produces the practitioner the hard assignments call for. The question is whether the friction is being maintained long enough for that practitioner to develop.

Chapter Three: What Real Understanding Looks Like

Tom is twenty-six, writes marketing copy, and uses AI to generate arguments for products he has been briefed on. The companion volume found him producing fluent, competent work that his employer accepts and his clients pay for, and lacking something that a marketing director caught immediately on a specific assignment: the argument had no center. The copy described. It did not persuade. The difference, the companion volume argued, is the difference between understanding argument structure and having the illusion of it.

This chapter is about Tom on the other path. About what it looks like when genuine understanding develops rather than its illusion. About what the aha moment is and how to create the conditions in which it happens. About the specific practices that build real understanding rather than fluent transmission.

The Transfer Test as a Development Tool

The companion volume described the transfer test as a diagnostic: can you apply what you learned to a situation that differs from the one in which you learned it? The test distinguishes genuine understanding from fluent recall. It is also, on the other path, a development tool.

A writer who constructs an argument from scratch, without AI scaffolding, and then applies that argument structure to a different subject is doing something that builds the structural understanding the transfer test measures. Not because the practice produces correct work immediately, it often does not, but because the attempt to transfer activates the structural knowledge in a way that reception does not. A writer who constructs an argument and applies it discovers where the structure holds and where it is specific to the original subject. That discovery is the learning.

Tom, on the other path, has developed a practice of writing argument sketches. Not full pieces. A paragraph that states a claim, a paragraph that makes the supporting argument, a paragraph that anticipates the strongest objection and addresses it. He does this without AI, on subjects he has been asked to write about, before the AI is consulted. The sketches are rough. They are often wrong in their logic. When they are wrong, he can see where the argument breaks down, which is information he would not have if the AI had scaffolded the argument for him.

The AI arrives after the sketch. He asks it: what is wrong with this argument? Where does it break down? What would a skeptical reader find most unconvincing? The AI's response is evaluated against the sketch he made. The gaps the AI identifies are gaps in his structural understanding that he can now see specifically rather than experiencing generically as "the copy is not persuasive." The specific gap is the learning target. Over time, the specific gaps have become fewer and the arguments have become more structurally sound, not because the AI improved them but because the practice of making and breaking arguments has built the structural knowledge that makes genuine persuasion possible.

The Aha Moment as a Practice

The aha moment, the neurologically distinct experience of genuine understanding arriving after a period of confusion, is not a random event. It has conditions that favor it and conditions that prevent it. Those conditions are the foundation of learning to produce genuine understanding rather than its illusion.

The conditions that favor the aha moment are: a prior period of genuine engagement with the material, during which the person formed their own model of how things work; a problem or contradiction that reveals a gap in that model; and enough time with the gap to feel its shape before the correct explanation arrives. The aha moment is the experience of the gap closing. Without the gap, there is no aha. Without the time with the gap, the closure does not consolidate in the way that makes it durable and transferable.

AI short-circuits the second and third conditions. It provides the correct explanation before the gap has been felt, which means the gap never forms, which means the aha never occurs, which means the understanding that arrives is the thin kind that passes tests and fades quickly. The companion volume documented this as damage. On the other path, it suggests a practice: engineer the conditions for the aha rather than accepting the conditions that prevent it.

The engineering is specific. Before consulting AI on a question the practitioner needs to understand genuinely: sit with the question long enough to form a wrong answer. Not a correct answer, the correct answer is what the AI will provide. A wrong answer that represents the practitioner's actual current model of the subject. The wrong answer is the gap made visible. The AI's correct response, compared to the wrong answer, produces the aha because there is now a gap for it to close.

This is Robert Bjork's desirable difficulty principle applied deliberately: introduce the failure before the correction so that the correction consolidates rather than slides off. The practitioner who has formed a wrong answer, received the correct explanation, and identified specifically where their model was wrong has learned something that will be available when the situation requires it. The practitioner who received the correct explanation without the wrong answer has information that will be unavailable at the moment of transfer.

The Expert's Edge and How It Develops

The companion volume described a capacity that genuine understanding produces and AI explanations cannot: the ability to recognize when something is wrong before you can articulate why. The experienced editor who knows the argument is off before identifying which sentence is wrong. The senior programmer who feels that the control flow is wrong before running the code.

This capacity has a name in cognitive science: chunking. The expert has encountered enough instances of correct and incorrect versions of patterns in their domain that the pattern itself becomes a unit of perception. They are not consciously evaluating individual elements. They are perceiving the pattern directly, the way a fluent reader perceives words rather than letters. The perception of a pattern that violates the learned schema produces the felt sense of wrongness before conscious analysis can locate it.

Chunking develops through exposure to many instances of the pattern, with feedback that allows the person to calibrate their perception against reality. The chess player who has seen ten thousand positions develops a perception of position quality that the beginner does not have. A writer who has read and revised ten thousand arguments develops a perception of argument quality that produces the editorial instinct. The programmer who has debugged ten thousand systems develops the diagnostic intuition that the companion volume described.

AI threatens this development in a specific way: it reduces the number of instances the practitioner processes with full attention. A writer who accepts AI-generated argument structures has not perceived those structures as an expert perceives them. They have read them, found them acceptable, moved on. The reading is not calibrating their perception against their own judgment. It is not producing the feedback loop that develops chunking. The instances are passing through without leaving the cognitive traces that expert pattern recognition requires.

The augmented practitioner, on the other path, maintains the instance count. Not by refusing AI assistance in every context, but by ensuring that enough instances pass through their own active evaluation, with their own prior judgment engaged, to keep the calibration process running. A writer who constructs argument sketches before AI is consulted is maintaining the instance count in the domain of argument structure. The programmer who forms a hypothesis before pasting an error is maintaining it in the domain of system diagnosis. The instances are fewer than the total instances processed with AI assistance, but they are the right kind, the kind where genuine evaluation is happening rather than acceptance.

Tom at twenty-six, on the current path, produces competent copy at high volume and does not know what he does not know. The marketing director who rejected the piece with no center knew something Tom did not know and could not see from where he was standing.

Tom at thirty-two, on the other path, has spent six years doing something that felt slower and was: writing argument sketches before AI, reviewing them against AI challenges, tracing the specific failures of his logic, rebuilding the argument when the failure was real and defending it when the AI's objection was wrong. The practice is not dramatic. It is twenty minutes at the start of each project before the AI is opened. Twenty minutes of forming a wrong model before the correct one is available.

At thirty-two, Tom has something. Not a credential or a title, though he has those too. He has a felt sense of how arguments work that produces the editorial instinct described above: the ability to read a brief and know, before he can articulate it, whether the argument will hold. His employers have noticed it. They call it good judgment. They are not wrong. It is good judgment. It is good judgment that was built through six years of practicing the cognitive work that AI was available to do for him, and that he chose to do himself, and that produced the specific competence that AI assistance alone cannot produce.

The marketing director who rejected Tom's piece at twenty-six had that same felt sense. It took her twelve years to build it. Tom at thirty-two, on the other path, has built the beginning of it in six years because the practice has been deliberate rather than incidental. The deliberate practice is the other path's efficiency advantage, and it is the only efficiency advantage the other path has. Everything else takes longer. The development does not.

Knowing What You Do Not Know

The companion volume argued that genuine understanding produces a capacity more valuable than correct answers: knowing what you do not know. A writer who truly understands argument structure knows where their argument has a gap. The programmer who genuinely understands a system knows which parts are uncertain and where the untested assumptions live.

This self-knowledge is not produced by receiving correct information. The experience of being wrong produces it in specific ways, enough times, in domains where the consequences of the wrongness are legible. The practitioner who has constructed arguments and had them fail, debugged systems and been wrong about the cause, worked through problems and discovered that their model was incorrect in a specific place: this practitioner has a calibrated sense of their own knowledge gaps. They know where to be confident and where to be careful. The calibration is the product of the experience of being wrong.

AI dependency removes this calibration because it removes the experience of being wrong. The practitioner who accepts AI-generated work and receives client approval has not received feedback about the quality of their own judgment. They have received feedback about the quality of the AI's output. The feedback does not calibrate their sense of their own limitations. It calibrates their sense of how useful the AI is, which is a different and less valuable kind of self-knowledge.

On the other path, the argument sketch practice produces exactly this calibration. Tom at thirty-two knows where his arguments tend to fail. He knows which kinds of objections he reliably anticipates and which he reliably misses. He knows the structural patterns his copy falls into that feel like logic but are not. This self-knowledge is the foundation of the good judgment his employers have noticed. It is not innate. It was built through the repeated practice of being wrong in a domain and having the wrongness be legible enough to learn from.

The Illusion Problem in the Other Direction

The companion volume was primarily concerned with the illusion of understanding: the experience of comprehension without its substance. The other path creates a different risk that is worth naming: the illusion of competence from deliberate practice alone, without the feedback that makes the practice calibrating.

Practice without accurate feedback produces confident wrong models. A writer who spends twenty minutes producing argument sketches and never receives challenge on those sketches may be reinforcing structural errors rather than correcting them. The programmer who forms hypotheses but never checks them against the correct diagnosis may be building a more confident wrong model rather than a more accurate one.

This is why the adversarial AI session is not optional on the other path. The practice of forming models independently is necessary but not sufficient. The models need to be tested against something that can identify their failures. The AI, used in the adversarial mode, is the testing mechanism. The sequence, form the model, test it against the AI, identify the specific gap, revise the model, is what produces calibration rather than confident incompetence.

What matters is that the AI is being used to test the practitioner's model, not to provide the model. The practitioner who uses AI to generate explanations of what they should have understood is receiving the model from outside. The practitioner who uses AI to challenge the model they have formed independently is testing something they own. Ownership is the condition for calibration. You cannot calibrate what you did not make.

Tom on the other path does both: he makes the argument, and he tests it. The making and the testing are both necessary. The making without the testing produces a practitioner who is confident but not accurate. The testing without the making produces a practitioner who has received a lot of correct information without the ownership that makes it durable. The sequence is the practice. The practice is the development. The development is the thing.

Chapter Four: The Classroom of Failure

Elena published a piece with a fabricated citation. Deon shipped authentication code with a session fixation vulnerability. Neither of them intended to fail. Both of them failed in ways that were invisible until they were not, because the AI's confident wrong outputs look identical to its confident correct ones, and neither of them had developed the domain-specific instinct for noticing the difference.

The companion volume treated these failures as costs. This chapter treats them as data. Not the failures Elena and Deon experienced, those were real and consequential and not recommended. The productive failures: the kind the augmented practitioner engineers deliberately, in conditions where the consequences are legible and the learning is available, before the real-world version arrives.

The augmented practitioner's relationship to failure is the inverse of the AI-dependent practitioner's. The AI-dependent practitioner avoids failure by outsourcing the work that would produce it. The augmented practitioner courts failure deliberately, in controlled conditions, because they understand that the wrong answer, when it is their wrong answer, is a mirror that shows them something about their own thinking that no correct answer can show.

The Wrong Answer as a Mirror

When you get something wrong, the wrong answer is specific. It is not random noise. It is the output of your actual current model of the subject, which means it reveals the specific error in that model. The fabricated citation

Elena accepted without checking revealed something specific about her verification habits: she was checking citations by plausibility rather than by source. The session fixation vulnerability Deon shipped revealed something specific about his security mental model: he was thinking about session validation as a single point rather than as a process with distinct stages.

Neither of them learned this about themselves from the failure, because the failure arrived after the work was done, in a context where the connection between the error and the model that produced it was not being examined. The failure was experienced as an external problem to be corrected rather than as information about an internal model to be revised.

The productive failure is different in structure. It is engineered so that the connection between the error and the model is visible. A writer who attempts a claim without AI assistance, has it challenged by the adversarial session, and identifies specifically where the claim rested on an assumption rather than evidence, has received the same information as Elena, that their verification was insufficient, in a form that directly illuminates the specific gap. The learning is available because the error and the model that produced it are both present and the practitioner is looking at both.

Deon on the other path runs security reviews of his own code before shipping, using a checklist of the specific failure modes he has been wrong about before. The checklist is not static. It is his personal catalog of the specific errors his mental model of security has produced over time. Each time a new error appears, either in his own work or in AI-generated code he is reviewing, it gets added to the catalog. The catalog is a map of his own failure modes. It is more useful than any generic security guide because it is calibrated to the specific ways his judgment goes wrong, rather than to the general ways that programmers in the abstract go wrong.

Engineering Productive Failure

Productive failure does not happen by accident in a professional environment that rewards correct outputs. It has to be engineered. The conditions that make failure productive are specific and require deliberate setup.

The first condition is low stakes. The failure that produces learning needs to happen in a context where the consequences of the failure are legible but not catastrophic. A writer who attempts an argument sketch in a notebook and gets it wrong has made a low-stakes failure. The model that produced the wrong argument is still present. The correction is still available. Nothing important has been damaged. The same model error, expressed in a published piece, is a high-stakes failure that may produce a correction but does not produce the conditions for calibrated learning, because the practitioner's attention is on the correction rather than on the model.

The second condition is legibility. The failure needs to reveal something specific about the practitioner's model rather than producing a generic outcome like "wrong." This requires that the practitioner have formed an explicit model before the failure occurred, a hypothesis, a sketch, an attempt, so that the failure can be compared against the model and the specific gap identified. The practitioner who accepted AI output and had it fail has not formed their own model. The failure is not legible to them because there is no internal model for it to reveal a gap in.

The third condition is retrieval. The failure needs to be encountered again, in different contexts, often enough to produce durable revision of the model. A single productive failure produces a single correction. The same failure pattern encountered in ten different contexts over a period of months produces a revised mental model that will not produce that failure again. This is why the personal catalog of failure modes, Deon's security checklist, is more useful than a single review. It is the mechanism for repeated retrieval of the specific failure pattern across enough contexts to produce genuine revision.

Elena on the Other Path

Elena on the other path did not stop using AI for research. She changed what she does after the AI produces a claim.

Before the AI is consulted, she writes down what she already knows about the question and what she would expect a reliable answer to look like. Not a full account, a few sentences of prior expectation. When the AI's response arrives, she compares it to her prior expectation. The comparison is productive in two directions. When the AI's response aligns with her prior, she has a starting point for verification: does the source say what the AI claims it says? When the AI's response contradicts her prior, she has a flag: one of the two models is wrong, and it is worth finding out which.

The practice produces verification that is targeted rather than uniform. Elena does not check every citation with the same intensity. She checks the ones where something about the response does not match her prior, and she checks them carefully. Her prior expectation is the instrument for detecting the discrepancy. The instrument only works if the prior exists. The prior only exists if she has formed it before the AI provides the answer. The sequence is the practice.

Over three years of this practice, Elena's prior expectations have become more accurate. Not because she is more knowledgeable in an abstract sense, she knows roughly as much as she knew three years ago, but because the practice of forming expectations and comparing them to verified information has calibrated her sense of what reliable claims in her domains look like. She catches the discrepancies faster. The instrument has been sharpened by use.

The fabrication she published at eight months into using AI would not get past her now, not because she is smarter but because her prior expectation for that domain would have flagged the specific implausibility of the fabricated study. Her calibrated sense of what the research in her domain shows would have produced a mild dissonance when the fabricated study appeared. The dissonance is the signal. The signal requires the prior. The prior requires the practice.

Confidence Calibration as a Skill

The companion volume identified the absence of calibrated confidence as one of AI's structural problems: the system presents every output with uniform fluency regardless of how reliable that output is. The augmented practitioner addresses this not by trying to change the AI's behavior but by developing their own calibrated confidence, which allows them to supply the uncertainty signal the AI does not provide.

Calibrated confidence is the skill of knowing how certain you should be about a claim given what you know about it. It is distinct from confidence in the colloquial sense, which is often disconnected from accuracy. A well-calibrated person who says they are eighty percent sure of a claim is right about eighty percent of the time when they use that level of confidence. A poorly calibrated person may say the same thing and be right forty percent of the time or ninety-five percent of the time, depending on the direction of their miscalibration.

Calibration is developed through feedback. You need to know how often you were right when you were eighty percent confident, and how often you were right when you were fifty percent confident, and whether those rates match your stated confidence levels. This feedback is available to the practitioner who forms explicit prior expectations before consulting external sources, because the comparison between the prior and the verified outcome is exactly the feedback required for calibration.

Elena's three-year practice is a calibration practice. She has been forming expectations about what reliable research in her domains looks like, comparing those expectations to verified sources, and tracking where her expectations were accurate and where they were not. The tracking is informal, she does not maintain a spreadsheet of her confidence levels, but the practice itself is producing the feedback that calibration requires. Her instrument is getting sharper because it is being used and compared to reality.

A writer who does not form prior expectations before consulting AI has no calibration data. Their sense of what reliable claims look like in their domain is not being compared to verified reality. It is being compared to AI outputs, which is a different and less useful comparison. The instrument is not being sharpened. It may be getting blunter, as the pattern recognition for AI-generated claims, plausible-sounding, smoothly written, confidently stated, gradually replaces the pattern recognition for reliable ones.

The Security Audit as a Practice Model

Deon's situation, the programmer who ships code with invisible security vulnerabilities because their review process assumes AI-generated code is likely correct, has a specific practice model on the other path that is worth examining because it generalizes beyond security work.

The security audit as practiced by experienced security engineers is a model of productive failure engineering. The auditor approaches code assuming that something is wrong and looking for it, rather than assuming the code is correct and looking for anomalies. The adversarial assumption is the mechanism that finds what a benign review misses. The auditor has a mental model of common failure modes and checks for them systematically, not because they expect to find all of them in this specific code, but because the practice of looking builds and maintains the mental model that allows intuitive detection over time.

Deon on the other path applies this logic to his regular development work. Before shipping any security-adjacent code, he runs the equivalent of a brief adversarial review: what are the three most likely ways this could be wrong, based on his personal catalog of failure modes? The review takes fifteen minutes. It catches things that a benign read would not catch, because a benign read is not looking for them. More importantly, the practice of looking for specific failure modes is maintaining and refining his mental model of security, so that the intuitive detection described in the companion volume, the felt sense that something is wrong before it can be articulated, is being built rather than left to develop by accident or not develop at all.

The generalizable principle: adversarial review of your own work, conducted with your personal catalog of failure modes, is a productive failure practice. It is not primarily about catching errors in the specific piece of work being reviewed. It is about maintaining the mental model that allows error detection to become intuitive over time. The specific errors caught are the immediate return. The maintained and refined mental model is the compound return.

When AI Failure Is Itself Informative

The companion volume noted that the AI's wrong answers are not useful self-knowledge for the practitioner: they are noise from a different system. This is correct as a statement about the AI's failures in isolation. It understates the value of AI failure when the practitioner has formed a prior expectation before the AI responds.

When Elena forms a prior expectation about what the research in her domain says, consults the AI, and finds a discrepancy, the discrepancy is informative regardless of which side is wrong. If the AI is wrong, she has caught a confabulation. If she is wrong, she has discovered a gap in her domain knowledge. Both outcomes produce learning that she would not have received if she had consulted the AI without the prior. The prior is what makes the AI's failure informative: it creates a standard against which the failure can be evaluated.

This is the mechanism by which AI, used on the other path, becomes a calibration tool rather than a replacement tool. The AI is not calibrating the practitioner by being right. It is calibrating the practitioner by producing a response that can be compared to the practitioner's own prior model. The comparison is the calibration, regardless of which model is correct. The practitioner who verifies the discrepancy and finds that the AI was wrong has confirmed their domain knowledge. The practitioner who verifies the discrepancy and finds that their prior was wrong has identified a gap. Both outcomes sharpen the instrument. Neither outcome is available without the prior.

Elena does not need AI to be unreliable for this practice to be useful. She needs AI to be what it is: variable in reliability, with no reliable signal distinguishing the reliable outputs from the unreliable ones. In that environment, the prior expectation is the practitioner's own signal. It is imperfect and it sharpens through use. It is the alternative to having no signal at all, which is the situation of the practitioner who consults AI without a prior and accepts the output as accurate because it reads as authoritative.

The Compound Return on Deliberate Failure

The augmented practitioner's relationship to failure is the foundation of their calibration, their domain expertise, and their intuitive detection capacity. None of these develop in a practitioner who outsources the work that would produce the failures.

The compound return is not visible in the short term. Elena at eight months into the prior expectation practice is catching more discrepancies than she was catching before, but she is not yet dramatically faster or more accurate than a careful journalist who relies on AI for research and checks everything uniformly. What differs is not yet in her outputs. It is in her instrument, which is sharpening.

Elena at four years has a domain instinct that the uniform-checker does not have. She checks faster because she checks targeted rather than uniform. She catches more because her instrument detects implausibility rather than just checking plausibility. The pieces she is assigned are harder because her editors have noticed that she handles ambiguous sources with judgment rather than caution. The compound return is in what she is being asked to do, which has become harder and more valued because the instrument she has been building is now visible in the quality of her work.

Deon at four years has a security intuition his peers who accepted AI-generated code throughout do not have. He is the person his team consults on security-adjacent architecture decisions, not because he studied more but because he built a mental model through deliberate practice that the others did not build through acceptance. The model produces the felt sense of wrongness that the companion volume described as the expert's edge. It was built through four years of fifteen-minute adversarial reviews and a personal catalog that now has entries for failure modes he did not know existed when he started it.

The classroom of failure is not a formal institution. It is the daily practice of forming expectations before consulting external sources, comparing those expectations to verified reality, cataloging the specific ways your model was wrong, and returning to those failure patterns in enough different contexts to revise the model rather than just correct the specific instance. The classroom is available to any practitioner who chooses to attend it. Most do not, because the alternative is faster and more immediately satisfying. The practitioner who attends it is building something the faster alternative cannot build: the calibrated judgment that the hard assignments call for.

Chapter Five: Holding the Leash

Here is what holding the leash looks like in my own work. I write a chapter of a novel, then I ask AI about the character arc, the plot, the rough spots, whether the structure is working. I have already done the creative work. The AI helps me evaluate it. For ghostwriting I ask it how the seams between chapters look, whether the transitions hold, whether the voice is consistent. The writing came from me. The AI is a tool I am pointing at a specific question. The moment I let it generate the chapter instead of reviewing the chapter, I have handed over the leash. That is the line. It is not a complicated line. It just requires that you know which side of it you are on.

Priya stopped arguing with the draft. That was the companion volume's account of what happened to her: she revised within the AI's structure rather than questioning whether the structure was sound, and the error that lived in the structure went undetected until a colleague found it after the draft was finished. She corrected the report. She did not substantially change her workflow. The correction was real. The structural change was not.

Priya on the other path did not stop using AI to help structure her analysis. She changed one thing: before the AI sees the question she is trying to answer, she writes down what she thinks the answer is. Not a full analysis. A position. A sentence or two that states her current view of the policy question, based on what she already knows, before the AI's framing is available to anchor her thinking.

This is the practice of epistemic sovereignty in its simplest form: own your position before consulting the system that will offer you one.

What Epistemic Sovereignty Actually Means

The companion volume introduced cognitive sovereignty as the right to develop and exercise your own reasoning capacity without systematic interference from external systems designed to replace it. The concept is worth unpacking on the other path because the rights framing, while accurate, does not tell you what the practice looks like from the inside.

Epistemic sovereignty is not the absence of external influence. Humans have always been influenced by the information environments they inhabit, by the sources they consult, by the arguments they encounter. The historian is influenced by the sources she reads. The scientist is influenced by the literature in her field. The policy analyst is influenced by the research she reviews. None of this is a failure of sovereignty. External influence is how knowledge develops.

Epistemic sovereignty is the condition in which the practitioner's own reasoning is the frame through which external influence is evaluated, rather than external influence being the frame through which the practitioner's reasoning is organized. The distinction is structural, not about quantity of external input. Priya without sovereignty consults the AI, receives a structure, and revises within the structure. Priya with sovereignty forms a position, consults the AI, and evaluates the AI's structure against her position. In both cases she uses AI and external sources extensively. In one case her own reasoning is primary and external input is filtered through it. In the other case external input is primary and her reasoning is applied to its revision.

The structural difference produces different outcomes when the external source is wrong. Priya without sovereignty, working within the AI's structure, inherits the structural error without the opportunity to detect it because detection requires standing outside the structure and evaluating it, which her workflow does not provide. Priya with sovereignty, evaluating the AI's structure against her own position, encounters the error as a discrepancy between the AI's framing and what she knows the legislative history says. The discrepancy is the signal. The signal requires sovereignty to detect.

The Colossus Problem in Reverse

The companion volume used Colossus: The Forbin Project as a frame for the epistemic authority transfer: the humans lose control not because Colossus overpowers them but because they hand it authority before they understand what they are handing. The leash is handed over incrementally, one small decision at a time, until the pattern is visible and the leash is running from the other end.

The augmented practitioner's relationship to AI is the Colossus problem solved: they hold the leash. Not by refusing to engage the system, Forbin's mistake was not linking the systems, it was doing so before understanding what he was linking. The augmented practitioner links extensively, consults the system continuously, uses its outputs at every stage of the work. They hold the leash by maintaining the prior position that allows them to evaluate whether the system's output is sound.

Holding the leash is not a metaphor for distrust. It is a metaphor for structure. The practitioner who holds the leash is the one whose judgment remains the final evaluative frame. The AI can produce better arguments, more comprehensive research, stronger counterexamples than the practitioner could produce alone. The practitioner evaluates all of it against their own reasoned position. The AI's output can update that position. It should, when the output is correct and the practitioner's prior was wrong. The update should be the result of genuine evaluation, not of displacement. There is a difference between changing your mind because an argument convinced you and changing your mind because a fluent structure replaced the space where your argument would have been.

Priya's Position Practice

The position practice Priya has developed over two years is specific enough to describe.

Before opening a new analysis project, she writes what she is calling a prior statement: a paragraph that describes her current view of the question, based on her existing knowledge of the policy domain, before any AI-assisted research begins. The prior statement is not required to be correct. It is required to be genuinely hers: her actual current assessment, not the assessment she thinks she should have, not the assessment that will be easiest to defend, not the assessment the AI would produce.

The prior statement becomes the lens through which the AI-assisted research is evaluated. When the research confirms her prior, she notes it and continues. When the research contradicts her prior, she pauses and examines the contradiction: is the AI's framing more accurate than her prior, or is her prior revealing a problem in the AI's framing? The examination requires her to engage with the specific question of which model is better supported. That engagement is the epistemic work. Without the prior, there is no examination. The AI's framing fills the space where her position would have been.

The prior statement practice has changed the quality of her analysis in a specific way that her colleagues have noticed but not named: her reports have positions. Not just conclusions, which any competent analyst can produce. Positions: views of the policy question that are genuinely arguable, that she is prepared to defend under challenge, that represent her own judgment rather than a synthesis of available perspectives. The difference between a position and a conclusion is the difference between a practitioner who has done the epistemic work and a practitioner who has processed the research.

Her colleague who caught the original legislative history error is no longer catching errors in her work, not because she is producing less output but because the prior statement practice is catching the structural errors before the reports leave her desk. The prior statement creates the standing-outside-the-structure that the error detection requires. Sovereignty is the precondition for catching your own mistakes.

Knowing the System You Are Using

Epistemic sovereignty is not only about maintaining a prior position. It is also about knowing what the system you are consulting is, what its constraints are, and whose interests those constraints serve.

The companion volume described the AI system's guardrails as encoding a set of values rather than a neutral standard, built by a specific group of people with specific interests in specific cultural contexts. This is not a criticism that requires rejecting AI tools. It is a description of a condition that requires understanding them. The practitioner who knows that the system they use has a specific value framework, a specific relationship with government and military organizations, a specific commercial interest in the conclusions it produces, is in a different epistemic position than the practitioner who does not know these things. Both use the tool. One uses it with accurate information about what it is.

Priya, as a policy analyst covering technology regulation, has done the fifteen minutes of research the companion volume suggested: she knows who built the tools she uses, what their stated values are, what their documented relationships with government and commercial interests are, and where those relationships create specific incentives that might shape what the system produces. This knowledge does not make her distrust the tools. It makes her apply more scrutiny in the specific areas where the system's interests might diverge from accurate analysis.

For a policy analyst covering AI regulation, this scrutiny is not optional. The system she uses for research is produced by the industry she is analyzing. The system has a commercial and political interest in how that analysis comes out. A practitioner without sovereignty might not notice this conflict. A practitioner with sovereignty treats it as a flag: in this domain specifically, her prior position needs to be more firmly held and the adversarial review of the AI's framing needs to be more searching. The system's interests and her analytical interests diverge here, and she needs to be the one whose interests shape the analysis.

Self-Reinforcing Authority and How to Break It

The companion volume described the self-reinforcing nature of epistemic authority transfer: once the practitioner has accepted an AI output and acted on it, choice supportive bias works to retroactively justify the trust they extended, strengthening the prior for trusting the next output. The transfer compounds.

The position practice is the mechanism for breaking this dynamic before it compounds. The prior statement is written before the AI's output is available, which means the prior cannot be influenced by the output it will be compared against. This is the specific design property that makes the practice effective: the prior has to be formed in the absence of the thing that will anchor it if it is not formed first.

The practitioner who attempts to form a prior after consulting the AI, or even after being told what the question is in a context where they expect to consult the AI immediately, is not performing the same operation. The prior that forms in the shadow of a forthcoming AI response is already being shaped by the expectation of that response. The genuine prior requires genuine independence from the system's framing, and independence requires sequence: your position first, the system's framing second.

This sounds simple. It is simple. The difficulty is not in understanding the principle but in maintaining the discipline when the AI is available immediately, when the efficiency of prompting first is compelling, and when the prior position is uncomfortable because it is uncertain and the AI's response will be confident. The moment of resistance is the moment before the first prompt, when the practitioner chooses to sit with their own uncertainty for long enough to form a position rather than resolving the uncertainty by importing the AI's confidence. That moment, maintained consistently over months and years, is what the sovereignty practice consists of.

When the AI Updates Your Prior

A clarification that is easy to misunderstand: maintaining a prior position is not the same as refusing to update it. The augmented practitioner updates their prior when the AI's response provides genuine grounds for updating. The update is the point. The prior position is not a fortress. It is a starting point that makes genuine updating possible.

Without a prior position, there is no genuine updating. There is only replacement: the AI's framing fills the space where a position would have been, and the practitioner works within that framing without being aware that a choice was made. The practitioner who starts with a prior and has it overturned by compelling evidence has genuinely changed their mind. The practitioner who started with no prior and has it filled by the AI's first response has not changed their mind. Their mind was never in the game.

Priya has updated her prior positions many times. On specific legislative history questions, the AI's research has revealed that her prior was based on outdated or partial information, and she has revised accordingly. On specific policy analysis questions, the AI's synthesis has included a consideration she had not weighted heavily enough, and her analysis has become more accurate as a result. These updates are genuine intellectual progress. They are possible because she had a prior position for the AI's response to update. Without the prior, there is no update, only displacement, and displacement does not feel like anything different from genuine learning, which is the most dangerous thing about it.

Sovereignty at the Professional Scale

The prior statement practice is an individual practice. Its effects at the professional scale are what make it worth the individual cost.

Priya's think tank produces analysis that informs policy. When Priya has sovereignty, the analysis reflects her genuine judgment about what the evidence shows, evaluated against her knowledge of the domain and her understanding of the AI system's limitations and interests. When she does not have sovereignty, the analysis reflects the AI's framing of what the evidence shows, filtered through her revision. These are not the same thing, and the difference matters in proportion to how much weight the analysis carries.

A policy field in which analysis practitioners with sovereignty produce is a field in which disagreement reflects genuine differences in judgment. The disagreements are productive: they surface real considerations, test real positions, produce real intellectual progress. A policy field in which analysis is produced primarily by practitioners without sovereignty is a field in which disagreement increasingly reflects different AI framings of similar questions. The disagreements may look the same from the outside but they are less productive because they are not rooted in the practitioners' own calibrated judgment.

The companion volume argued that democratic deliberation requires a population capable of governing itself, and that the AI dependency trajectory threatens this capacity at the population level. The augmented practitioner's sovereignty practice is the individual contribution to maintaining the epistemic infrastructure that democratic deliberation requires. Not because one practitioner's sovereignty changes the population-level trajectory, but because the population-level trajectory is made of individual practices accumulated. Priya's prior statement, maintained consistently across hundreds of analysis projects, is one node of the epistemic infrastructure. The infrastructure is built from nodes. The nodes are built from practices. The practices are chosen by people.

Part Two: How It Gets Built

Chapter Six: The Long Development Arc

The companion volume traced the long erosion: forty years of technological change steadily reducing the cognitive demands placed on ordinary practitioners, softening the ground for AI's particular form of damage. Television reduced the demand for sustained engagement. Search engines reduced the demand for retention. Smartphones reduced sustained attention. Social media rewarded the performance of thinking over thinking itself. AI arrived into a population already primed for cognitive outsourcing, and the priming made the outsourcing faster and deeper than it would have been otherwise.

This chapter traces the arc in the other direction: the long development that produces the augmented practitioner. It is not a quick arc. The capacities described in Part One: genuine understanding, calibrated confidence, and epistemic sovereignty, do not develop in months. They develop over years, through practices maintained against the grain of environments that do not reward them, building something that is invisible in individual instances and unmistakable in the aggregate.

The long development arc is not romantic. It does not produce a finished product or a destination. It produces a practitioner who is more capable at forty than at thirty, more capable at thirty than at twenty-five, not because time passed but because specific practices were maintained through the time. The arc is made of daily choices, most of them small, most of them unnoticed, all of them compounding.

What Wikipedia Got Right

The companion volume added Wikipedia to the historical arc of cognitive erosion as an exception that confirmed the rule: a technology that required active contribution rather than passive consumption, that created cognitive demands rather than reducing them, that produced genuine expertise in its serious contributors because the platform's structure required real intellectual work to participate meaningfully.

Wikipedia's lesson is not that the internet is fine or that cognitive erosion is not happening. It is a lesson about mechanism: the trajectory of erosion is a product of incentive structure, not of technology. The platforms that invited passive consumption produced passive consumers. The platform that invited active contribution produced active contributors. The technology was the same technology. What differed was what the platform required of its users.

The augmented practitioner applies this lesson at the individual level. They design their own relationship to AI tools with the Wikipedia principle in mind: what does the tool require of me, and is what it requires the thing that develops me? When the answer is yes, when the tool requires genuine evaluation of its outputs against a prior position, when it requires adversarial engagement rather than passive acceptance, when it requires the practitioner to form something before the tool produces something, the tool is functioning like Wikipedia: as an invitation to active contribution rather than passive consumption. When the answer is no, the practitioner adjusts the relationship until it is.

The mechanism of the long development arc is the same as the mechanism of Wikipedia's success: active contribution, maintained consistently, across enough instances to produce genuine expertise. The augmented practitioner is contributing actively to the epistemic work their tools would otherwise do for them. The contribution is the development. There is no other development available.

The Spaced Return

Robert Bjork's research on spaced practice, the finding that spacing out practice sessions produces more durable retention than massing them, has a less-discussed implication for the augmented practitioner: the return to a domain after an interval is itself a productive difficulty. The practitioner who has not engaged with a problem domain for two weeks and then returns to it is not in the same cognitive state as the practitioner who has been engaging with it continuously. The return requires reconstruction of the domain model from memory, and that reconstruction is learning in a form that continuous engagement does not produce.

AI makes the spaced return less common and less necessary. The practitioner who consults AI can produce competent domain engagement at any time without the reconstruction that the spaced return requires. The consultation substitutes for the reconstruction. The substitution is efficient. The substitution also eliminates the learning that the reconstruction produces.

On the other path, the spaced return is protected. Before consulting AI on a question in a domain the practitioner has not engaged with recently, they write what they currently remember about the relevant considerations: their current model of the domain, with whatever gaps the interval has produced. The gaps are the point. The gaps reveal what the practitioner has retained from previous engagement and what needs to be reconstructed. The reconstruction, filling the gaps through their own thinking before the AI provides the answer, is the learning event. The AI then confirms, corrects, or extends the reconstruction. The combination of attempted reconstruction and external verification produces more durable domain knowledge than either alone.

Depth Before Breadth

The AI environment rewards breadth. A practitioner who uses AI competently can engage with an enormous range of domains, producing plausible outputs across all of them, without the deep knowledge of any particular domain that took years to build in previous generations. The breadth is real. The outputs are often adequate. The problem is that adequate breadth without depth does not produce the capacities that the hard assignments require: the novel case analysis, the counterintuitive insight, the creative solution to a problem no one has solved in quite the same way before.

The augmented practitioner makes a different trade. Not breadth at the expense of depth, but depth in a domain or two, with AI-assisted breadth where breadth is sufficient and depth is not required. A writer who has genuine deep expertise in one domain, who has read the primary sources, traced the arguments across years of literature, developed opinions that are genuinely hers and not synthesized from the surface, produces something in that domain that AI breadth cannot replicate. The AI-assisted breadth serves her by making the research across adjacent domains more efficient. The depth is the irreplaceable part.

The long development arc, for the augmented practitioner, is primarily an arc of deepening. Not accumulating more topics but going further into fewer topics, building the structural knowledge and calibrated confidence and chunking-based intuition that depth produces. The AI handles the breadth. The practitioner handles the depth. The division is not arbitrary. It reflects what each is good at. AI is very good at breadth. Human practitioners, when developed through years of genuine engagement with a domain, are very good at depth. The augmented practice keeps each in its proper place.

The Development Timeline

The augmented practitioner's development does not proceed in a straight line, and it is worth being honest about what different stages of the arc feel like from the inside, because the early stages feel like regression and the regression is part of the process.

In the first six months of maintaining the practices described in Part One, most practitioners find the work harder and their output worse than it was with full AI assistance. The prior statement practice is slow. The argument sketch produces rough work that is clearly inferior to what the AI would have produced. The adversarial session is uncomfortable in ways that the cooperative session is not. The spaced return produces gaps that are embarrassing to confront. Nothing in the first six months produces an obvious improvement in output quality.

This is the correct observation and the wrong conclusion. The practices are not producing better outputs in the first six months. They are producing better instruments. The argument sketch is calibrating the practitioner's sense of what a good argument looks like. The adversarial session is sharpening the practitioner's sense of where their thinking is weak. The spaced return is building the domain model that will eventually produce the intuition. The instrument improvement is real and invisible. The output improvement is delayed and unmistakable when it arrives.

At twelve to eighteen months, most practitioners who have maintained the practices begin to notice something changing in their speed at the specific tasks the practices target. The argument sketches come faster. The gaps in the spaced returns are smaller. The adversarial session produces fewer objections that they had not already considered. The instrument is visibly sharper in the domains where the practices have been most consistent.

At three years, the practices have become less effortful. The prior statement is a habit rather than a discipline. The argument sketch is the natural first move rather than a deliberate imposition on a workflow that would prefer to prompt first. The adversarial session is sought rather than required. The practitioner is using the tools in the way that produces development as a matter of course rather than as a conscious choice against the grain. This is when the compound return begins to be visible in the work itself: in the quality of the angles, the soundness of the arguments, the depth of the domain knowledge, the reliability of the calibration.

The timeline is not fixed. It depends on how often the practices are performed, in how many contexts, against how much genuine challenge. The practitioner who performs the argument sketch once a week is on a slower development arc than the practitioner who performs it daily. The practitioner who performs it daily in one domain is on a slower arc than the practitioner who performs it across multiple domains. Consistent practice across multiple contexts is what produces the transferable expertise rather than the domain-specific competence.

The Practitioner Who Started Late

If you are twenty years old reading this, here is what I want to say directly: AI is a vital part of your life whether you engage with it consciously or not. You must learn to use it or you will be left behind. That is not a threat. It is arithmetic. The people who learn to use these tools well will be more productive, better informed, and more capable than those who do not. But the key is using it as a tool, not a crutch. A crutch holds you up when you cannot walk. A tool extends what you can already do. The generation that figures out the difference will be the one that inherits something worth having.

The companion volume was primarily concerned with the generation that will not have a baseline to return to: the writers and programmers developing their careers now, in an environment where AI has been available from near the beginning, who may not have the experiential foundation that makes rehabilitation faster.

The long development arc is available to this generation too, but it looks different. For the practitioner who has five years of AI-assisted work and limited prior-AI experience, the arc does not begin with rehabilitation. It begins with foundation building. The practices described in Part One are not returning them to something they had before. They are building something they have not yet had.

Foundation building is slower than rehabilitation. The practitioner who had ten years of genuine domain engagement before AI can return to the instincts built during those years. The practitioner who has had two years of AI-assisted work is building from a smaller base. The arc is longer. The endpoint is the same.

The specific implication for younger practitioners: start the practices earlier rather than later. Every year of AI-assisted work without the prior statement practice, without the argument sketch, without the adversarial session, without the spaced return, is a year of output without development. The outputs are real. The development that would have accompanied the outputs is not happening. It is not lost forever, the practices can begin at any point, but the compound return on earlier investment is larger than the compound return on later investment, and the compounding starts when the practice starts and not before.

What the Long Arc Looks Like From Outside

The augmented practitioner at year three and the AI-dependent practitioner at year three look similar from outside in most professional contexts. Both produce adequate work. Both meet deadlines. Both have professional relationships and career trajectories that appear roughly equivalent.

What differs is visible in specific moments. The assignment with no template. The question that requires genuine judgment rather than synthesis. The client who wants to know what you think, not what the research shows. The system that fails in a way no one has seen before. The analysis that requires holding a complex position under challenge from people who disagree. In these moments, the practitioner on the long development arc has something to bring. The practitioner who has been optimizing for output has something to generate.

The difference compounds. The augmented practitioner gets the hard assignments because they handle the hard assignments well. The hard assignments are the ones that develop the practitioner further. The development produces the capacity for harder assignments still. The arc steepens over time for the practitioner who is on it, and flattens for the practitioner who is not.

At year ten, the divergence is visible from any professional vantage point. The practitioner who has been building has a reputation, a set of capabilities, and a professional positioning that the practitioner who has been outputting cannot replicate quickly. The reputation is built from the hard assignments handled well. The capabilities are built from the years of practices maintained. The positioning is the result of being the person who can be called for the thing that requires more than competent output.

The long arc is the answer to the question the companion volume asked but did not answer: what are you building? The augmented practitioner is building a practitioner. One who will be different at forty than at thirty, genuinely more capable rather than just more experienced, because the development arc they chose produced compound growth rather than plateau. The choice is available. The arc begins the day the practices begin. The compounding starts from that day.

Chapter Seven: Designing for Growth

The companion volume described the AI tool market as running a selection process: the products that survive are the ones that maximize adoption and retention, which means the products that are most immediately useful to the users most willing to offload cognitive work. The products that would develop users rather than just serve them are commercially disadvantaged against those that simply give users what they want immediately. The market does not produce design for minds. It produces design for adoption.

This chapter is about design for growth: what tools optimized for user development rather than user satisfaction would look like, what evidence exists that such tools are possible, and what the augmented practitioner can do in the meantime with the tools that exist.

The gap between what is possible and what exists is real. The market mechanism that produces the gap is not going to close it on its own. The augmented practitioner does not wait for the gap to close. They design their own relationship to the existing tools to extract the development that the tools do not provide by default.

What Design for Growth Requires

A tool designed for growth has properties that are the inverse of the properties that drive adoption.

It introduces productive friction at the points where productive difficulty would develop the user. It asks before it answers. It requires the user to demonstrate their own model of the problem before it provides the solution. It calibrates its level of scaffolding to the user's demonstrated ability, providing more when the user is genuinely stuck and less when the user's own capability is adequate to the task. It measures its success by what the user can do without it after the interaction, not by whether the interaction was satisfying.

These properties are not technically difficult to implement. The AI systems that currently exist are capable of asking before answering, of requiring a prior position before producing a structure, of calibrating scaffolding to demonstrated user capability. The difficulty is not technical. It is commercial: every one of these properties reduces short-term user satisfaction, which reduces adoption, which reduces the product's competitive position in a market that selects primarily on adoption.

The Anthropic-Pentagon standoff described in the companion volume demonstrated that principled design under commercial pressure is possible: a company can pay a real commercial cost for design choices that reflect genuine values rather than market optimization. It also demonstrated how unusual that is. The tools designed for growth will exist at the margin of the market, produced by practitioners or researchers or institutions with incentives different from the mainstream commercial AI market, until the regulatory or cultural environment changes the commercial calculation.

The Diamond Age Primer and What It Would Take

Neal Stephenson's The Diamond Age imagines an educational tool, the Young Lady's Illustrated Primer, that is designed explicitly for development rather than delivery. The Primer does not tell Nell the answers to the problems she faces. It presents her with situations calibrated to her current level, waits for her to engage with them, provides feedback that develops her capacity to handle the next harder situation, and adjusts its challenges as she grows. The Primer is a tool that makes its user more capable precisely because it refuses to make things easy when making things easy would prevent growth.

The Primer is fiction. The reason it remains fiction is commercial rather than technical. A system that withholds the answer when the user is capable of finding it, that introduces friction when the user would prefer resolution, that measures success by the user's eventual independence rather than their continued engagement, would lose the market competition to systems that simply answer immediately. The market rewards engagement. The Primer produces independence. Independence reduces engagement. The market cannot currently price the value of the independence it produces.

The evidence that the Primer's design philosophy is technically achievable exists in educational contexts where the commercial pressure is different. AI tutoring systems that implement Socratic scaffolding, withholding direct answers, prompting the student toward the solution, calibrating the level of scaffold to demonstrated understanding, produce better learning outcomes than systems that provide direct answers. They exist. They are not winning the mainstream market because they are harder to use in the short term and the short term is what most users evaluate.

The augmented practitioner who understands this is in a position to implement the Primer's design philosophy in their own relationship to the tools they use. Not by waiting for the tools to be redesigned. By using the existing tools in ways that impose the productive friction the tools do not impose by default.

Retrofitting Friction

The practices described in Part One are, in structural terms, a retrofit of the productive friction that design for growth would build into the tools by default. The prior statement practice imposes the "ask before answering" property that the tool does not impose. The argument sketch imposes the "require the user's model before providing the solution" property. The adversarial session imposes the "measure by what the user can do" property. The spaced return imposes the calibration of scaffold to demonstrated capability.

The retrofit is less efficient than the designed-in version would be. A tool that automatically asked for the user's prior model before providing a solution would impose the sequence without requiring the user to remember to impose it. A tool that automatically calibrated its scaffold to demonstrated user capability would adjust the level of challenge without requiring the user to consciously manage the adjustment. The designed-in version produces development through normal use. The retrofit requires deliberate, sustained effort to maintain the sequence against the grain of a tool that would prefer to skip it.

The deliberate effort is the cost of the other path in the current environment. It is real and it is ongoing. The augmented practitioner accepts it because they understand what the alternative produces: fast, frictionless work that builds nothing except the output and the habit of needing the tool to produce the output. The retrofit is slower. It builds the practitioner. The choice between those two outcomes is the choice at the center of both volumes.

Tools That Reward Judgment

Not all existing AI tools are equally hostile to development. There is variation in the current market, and part of designing for growth is choosing the tools that, even within the commercial constraints, are more aligned with development than others.

The tools that most reward judgment over acceptance are the tools that produce incomplete outputs, that present options rather than conclusions, that ask questions rather than providing answers. The code generation tool that produces a partial implementation and annotates what it has not implemented, and why, is more compatible with augmented practice than the tool that produces a complete implementation without explanation. The writing tool that produces an outline with explicit flags for where the argument is weak is more compatible than the tool that produces a polished draft.

The augmented practitioner also chooses how to use any given tool in ways that increase the tool's compatibility with development. The same code generation tool can be used to generate a complete implementation that the practitioner accepts, or to generate an implementation that the practitioner was going to build anyway and now evaluates against their own design. The tool is the same. The use is different. The first use reduces the practitioner's cognitive engagement with the problem. The second extends it by providing a concrete artifact to evaluate.

The evaluation mode is the augmented practitioner's default orientation to AI outputs. Not acceptance, not rejection, but evaluation: comparing the output to a prior standard and identifying specifically where it meets the standard, where it exceeds it, and where it fails to. The evaluation requires a prior standard. The prior standard requires the practitioner to have engaged with the problem before the AI did. The engagement is the development. The evaluation is the mechanism that makes the development compound.

What Nina Could Have Built

The companion volume followed Nina, a programming tutorial creator who decided not to make a security vulnerability series because the platform's guardrail system made the content economically unviable. The chilling effect was real: content that would have been legitimately valuable was not created because the incentive structure made creating it too expensive.

Nina on the other path did not make the series for the platform. She made it for herself. Not as published content, the platform economics had not changed, but as a deliberate practice: working through the security vulnerability patterns she had been planning to document, building the implementations, writing the explanations, developing the pedagogical sequence that would have structured the series. The work produced no views, no revenue, no professional exposure.

It produced something else. After two years of working through security patterns as a personal practice, implementing the vulnerabilities, tracing the attack vectors, building the fixes, Nina had a security knowledge that her peers who had been creating AI-assisted content about security patterns did not have. The difference was not in what she knew about security in the abstract. It was in what she had built, implemented, and seen fail. The personal practice that the platform economics did not reward built the expertise that the market for senior security-adjacent development work does reward.

The lesson is not that economic incentives do not matter. They do. The lesson is that the practices that develop the augmented practitioner are not always the practices that the current incentive structure rewards, and waiting for the incentive structure to reward the right practices is waiting for the market mechanism to produce what it is structurally unable to produce. The practice happens outside the incentive structure, as a separate investment in the practitioner's own development, or it does not happen.

The Standard Worth Demanding

The companion volume described three design changes that would make a measurable difference in AI tools if implemented: a default mode that asks before generating, calibrated uncertainty markers that distinguish high-confidence outputs from low-confidence ones, and a session summary that shows what the user contributed versus what the AI generated. None of these have been implemented by any major AI product.

The augmented practitioner does not wait for the implementation. They implement the equivalent through their own practice. The prior statement is the personal version of "ask before generating." The verification practice is the personal version of calibrated uncertainty.

The session review described in the companion volume, three minutes at the end of a work session noting where the practitioner did the thinking versus where the AI did, is the personal version of the session summary.

These personal implementations are less efficient than the designed-in versions would be. They require effort to maintain. They do not scale to everyone who uses AI tools, because most people will not maintain them without structural support. What they do is demonstrate, in the practitioner's own experience, that the alternative to the current default is possible and produces the outcomes it claims to produce. The demonstration is the beginning of the demand. The practitioners who have experienced the compound return on design for growth are the people who have standing to demand it from the tools they use. The demand accumulates as the practitioners who have made the other path work begin to describe what it has produced.

The standard worth demanding is not complicated: design that treats user cognitive development as a metric worth measuring, alongside the engagement and satisfaction metrics that currently dominate. A tool that knows whether its users are becoming more capable over time at the tasks the tool assists with is a tool with a different in kind relationship to its users than a tool that only knows whether users return tomorrow. The first tool has an interest in its users' development. The second tool has an interest in its users' continued need. The augmented practitioner, on the other path, is building a relationship with tools that is closer to the first kind, regardless of whether the tools themselves have been designed to enable it.

Chapter Eight: Teaching Thinking Again

The companion volume's account of education was bleak and accurate. The accountability-driven system that preceded AI had already oriented itself away from the development of independent thinking and toward the production of measurable outputs. AI arrived to find the gates open and a welcome committee. The institution that should have been building the foundation was already dismantling it, and AI made the dismantling faster and easier to sustain.

This chapter is not a policy proposal for reforming the education system. The companion volume was honest that the political economy of education reform runs against every intervention that would work. The structural constraints are real. The institutional inertia is real. The timeline on which genuine reform operates is longer than the timeline on which AI is reshaping cognitive development.

What this chapter is about: the specific practices that develop genuine thinking, why they work, and where they can be implemented now by the people who have the will and the standing to implement them. Not everywhere. Not at the scale the problem requires. In the classrooms and households and mentoring relationships where individual choice can still determine what develops and what does not.

What Writing Was Actually For

The companion volume described the five-paragraph essay as the prototype of AI-generated writing: a structure that can be learned and applied without genuine understanding, that rewards the performance of intellectual work over the actual cognitive effort that produces original thinking. This description is accurate about the five-paragraph essay as it is currently taught. It is not accurate about writing as a thinking technology, which is what the essay was before accountability systems reduced it to a format.

Writing is thinking made visible and therefore correctable. A writer who attempts to articulate a position in prose discovers, in the attempt, whether the position is coherent. The argument that seemed clear in the head reveals its gaps when it has to be written out. The claim that felt supported turns out to rest on an assumption that the writer had not examined. The structure that seemed logical produces a paragraph that does not connect to the one before it, which reveals that the logical connection did not exist.

This is what the essay was for. Not as a format to be evaluated for correctness. As a process through which the writer's thinking is externalized, examined, and made more precise. The evaluation was supposed to assess the quality of the thinking the process produced. The accountability system evaluated the format instead, which eliminated the thinking without eliminating the format.

The teacher who understands this can still use writing as a thinking technology even within the accountability system, by designing writing assignments that require the externalization and examination of the student's actual thinking rather than the demonstration of format competence. The in-class freewrite before any research. The position paper that requires defending a view the student holds rather than synthesizing views from provided sources. The revision assignment that requires the student to explain specifically what was wrong with their first draft and why the revision is better. None of these require abandoning the accountability system. They require using the essay as the thinking technology it was supposed to be.

The Socratic Method Is Not Obsolete

The Socratic method was displaced by the accountability system because it does not scale, cannot be standardized, and its outcomes are difficult to measure. These are genuine disadvantages. They do not make it obsolete. They make it unavailable at the scale the problem requires and available at the scale of the individual teacher, tutor, parent, or mentor who chooses to use it.

The Socratic method works against AI dependency for a reason that is precise and worth stating: it cannot be shortcut by AI. When a teacher asks a student to defend their position in real time, to respond to a challenge rather than revise their written answer, they are creating a situation in which the student must engage with the question independently. The AI is not present in the conversation. The student's thinking, whatever they have, is the only resource available. The conversation reveals what that thinking is, not what the AI produced.

A student who has been through genuine Socratic instruction has a different relationship to their own positions than the student who has not. They have experienced the difference between a position that holds under examination and one that collapses when challenged. They know what it feels like to have an argument work and to have it fail. This experiential knowledge cannot be transmitted by reading about Socratic method or watching a video about critical thinking. It is produced by the experience of thinking under pressure, with feedback, from someone who is genuinely challenging rather than confirming.

The teacher who uses Socratic method effectively has specific characteristics: comfort with silence, tolerance for partially right answers, ability to ask the question that advances the student's thinking rather than providing the answer the teacher wants to hear. These characteristics are teachable. They are not currently being taught in most teacher training programs, which are oriented toward the accountability system's preference for measurable, reproducible instructional methods. The individual teacher who develops them is working against the grain of their professional training. Those teachers exist. Their students are different.

Assignments That AI Cannot Replace

The most productive reframing of the AI-in-education question is not about detection or prohibition but about design. What kinds of assignments are genuinely difficult to complete with AI assistance in ways that satisfy the assignment's developmental purpose? Not difficult to complete, AI can complete almost any assignment. Difficult to complete in ways that satisfy the purpose of building the student's thinking.

Oral defense of written work. A student who submits an AI-generated piece cannot defend it in a twenty-minute conversation with an instructor who probes the reasoning, asks for elaborations that do not appear in the text, and requires the student to explain what they would have argued differently. The oral defense exposes the gap between the writing and the writer. It cannot be prepared for with AI assistance because the preparation would require the student to understand the argument, at which point the gap has been closed and the defense has served its developmental purpose.

Debugging intentionally broken code written by someone else. This requires reading another programmer's logic, identifying where it fails, and articulating why. AI can assist with this task but cannot replace the student's engagement with it, because the engagement is what the task is measuring: the student's ability to read code they did not write, hold its logic in working memory, and identify the specific failure. The skill is the process. The AI can suggest where to look, but the looking itself is the development.

The in-class timed write. Fifteen minutes on a question the student has not seen before, with no AI access, producing a paragraph that demonstrates what they can do independently. The paragraph does not have to be polished. It has to be the student's own work under constraint. The constraint is the assessment condition and the development condition at the same time: the student who practices producing something genuine under time pressure is building the capacity that the blank page requires.

The revision assignment with accountability. Not "revise this draft" but "revise this draft and explain specifically what was wrong with the original, why the revision is better, and what you understand now that you did not understand when you wrote the first version." The accountability requirement forces genuine engagement with the revision rather than the substitution of a better AI-generated draft for a worse one. The explanation of what changed and why is the thinking that the revision was supposed to produce.

Fatima's Teacher

Fatima is sixteen and has never written substantial analytical work without AI assistance. The companion volume found her in a structural position where the AI dependency was invisible as a problem because she had no experiential baseline for what independent thinking at full development feels like. She does not know what she is missing.

Fatima has a teacher. That teacher is making choices right now that will matter for Fatima regardless of what the institution around them does. The teacher who requires the ten-minute in-class write before any AI-assisted work is creating, for Fatima, the experience of attempting something without the tool. The attempt does not have to produce good work. It has to be genuine. The genuine attempt is Fatima's first encounter with her own thinking as a thing that exists and can be developed.

The teacher who then uses Fatima's in-class write as the starting point for a Socratic conversation, asking her what she meant by a specific phrase, why she chose that framing rather than another, what she would say to someone who disagreed with her position, is giving Fatima the experience of thinking under examination. The examination is not hostile. It is the teacher genuinely interested in the student's thinking, helping her discover what she believes and why. This experience is not available from AI. The AI confirms. The Socratic teacher challenges. This challenge is the development.

This teacher faces pressure. Fatima's in-class writes are rougher than the polished AI-assisted submissions from other classes. The Socratic conversations take longer than direct instruction. The grades on unassisted work are lower than grades on AI-assisted work, and grades are what everyone is measuring. The teacher who holds the standard despite the pressure, who treats the lower grade on the in-class write as information about where Fatima is rather than as evidence that the assignment was unfair, is doing something that the accountability system does not reward and that matters anyway.

James's Instructor

James is nineteen, in his second year of a computer science degree, struggling in data structures in ways that confuse him because he passed introductory programming with high marks. The companion volume identified the gap: his introductory grades reflected AI-assisted output quality, not his foundational understanding. The data structures course requires the foundation. The foundation was not built.

James has an instructor. The instructor can see the gap between James's introductory grades and his data structures performance, and has two options for framing it. The first framing: James is struggling because he is not working hard enough or is not suited for computer science. The second framing: James is struggling because his introductory experience did not build the foundational understanding the current course requires, and the mismatch is a curriculum design problem rather than a student ability problem.

The instructor who adopts the second framing has a different conversation with James. Not "you need to study more" but "let's find where your mental model breaks down and rebuild it from there." The rebuilding requires the instructor to do something that is time-intensive and not rewarded by the standard metrics: to work with James through problems at a level of specificity that reveals the specific place where his model is wrong, then to help him correct the model rather than the problem.

This is tutoring in the deepest sense, and it is what the Mentat training described in the companion volume looks like at the level of an individual student and an individual instructor. The instructor who does this for James is doing it at a cost in time and without institutional reward. They are doing it because they understand that James's gap is a gap in the foundational understanding that the course assumes was built in the prerequisite, and that sending James forward without closing the gap produces a programmer who cannot debug systems he did not write from scratch, which is most of the actual programming work that exists.

What Parents Can Do Right Now

The companion volume described what parents can do outside the school system and it is worth spelling out what the practice looks like day to day.

The most important thing is not limitation. It is modeling. The parent who uses AI in front of their child in the adversarial mode, asking AI to challenge their position, disagreeing with AI's response, explaining to the child why the AI's argument did not convince them, is demonstrating that the relationship to AI is evaluative rather than receptive. The child who has seen this demonstration knows that consulting AI is not the same as having an answer, that the consultation is the beginning of a reasoning process rather than the end of it, that the person consulting the AI has and maintains a position of their own.

The requirement of the unassisted attempt before the AI-assisted version is valuable precisely because it is a requirement rather than a suggestion. The child who is required to write a paragraph before opening the AI does not have the option of skipping the uncomfortable stage. The requirement creates the experience the parent is trying to provide. The suggestion creates the option to avoid it, and most children, like most adults, will avoid the uncomfortable thing when the comfortable alternative is immediately available.

The conversation about what AI is, a system that produces statistically likely text rather than verified fact, that has guardrails built by specific people with specific interests, that is confident regardless of accuracy, is not a technical lecture. It is a short explanation that a twelve-year-old can understand and that changes their relationship to AI outputs for the rest of their life. The child who understands that AI produces what sounds right rather than what is right is in a categorically different epistemic position from the child who does not. The explanation takes five minutes. The position change is permanent.

Teaching thinking is not primarily about method. It is about the sustained practice of requiring genuine thinking from the specific people in your sphere, explaining why you are requiring it, and demonstrating through your own behavior that genuine thinking is something you value and practice yourself. The teacher who requires the in-class write. The instructor who rebuilds the foundation rather than passing the student forward. The parent who models the adversarial mode. These people are the sites where teaching thinking is happening. The institution is not the site. The individual is the site.

Chapter Nine: Who Should Pull the Levers

Trust the tech companies and the regulators to get this right? No. The answer to who should pull the levers in education is straightforward: teachers and students. Not corporate product managers, not policy consultants, not the companies that sell the tools. The people in the room. And here is something most reform efforts miss: if you involve the students in the decisions, they buy into the outcome. Students who help design the rules around AI use in their classroom are students who have already thought through the tradeoffs. That process is itself an education in the thing this book is arguing for. The governance of AI in education should not flow down from technology companies. It should build up from the people doing the learning.

The companion volume mapped the governance terrain honestly. A handful of companies control the cognitive infrastructure of civilization. The democratic institutions that should govern them are slower than the technology and increasingly dependent on the industry for the expertise to regulate it. The geopolitical competition provides a justification for speed that is difficult to argue against. The open source question has no clean answer. The regulatory capture is already underway.

The companion volume also described one thing that cut against the general direction of that terrain: the Anthropic-Pentagon standoff. A company that accepted a real commercial cost for holding a principled position against enormous pressure. Not evidence that the system is fine. Evidence that principled behavior under structural pressure is possible, is rarer than it should be, and is worth understanding because the understanding changes what the augmented practitioner can do with it.

This chapter is about the governance question from the inside: not who currently pulls the levers and why, but what it would look like if the levers were pulled with genuine accountability to the people affected, what the augmented practitioner can do to move the arrangement in that direction, and what the specific practices of civic engagement look like when the practitioner has maintained the cognitive sovereignty that effective civic engagement requires.

The Anthropic Question

The Anthropic-Pentagon standoff is worth examining on the other path because it illustrates both the possibility and the cost of principled design under structural pressure, and the augmented practitioner needs to understand both.

Anthropic held its position on autonomous weapons and mass surveillance restrictions when the Pentagon demanded their removal, when the Trump administration blacklisted the company, when OpenAI announced a deal on the terms Anthropic had refused within days of the blacklisting. The cost was real and immediate: lost government revenue, a federal supply-chain risk designation, reputational attack. The position held.

The lesson the augmented practitioner takes from this is not that Anthropic is a good company deserving of uncritical support. The companion volume was clear that Anthropic's design is not fully consistent with design-for-minds principles, that its system still optimizes substantially for user satisfaction in ways that produce dependency rather than development. The lesson is structural: a company can pay a real price for a principle and still hold it. That this is unusual in the AI industry does not make it theoretical. It is demonstrated.

The augmented practitioner's response to this demonstration is not to trust Anthropic but to understand it as evidence that the incentive structure does not determine every outcome. The structural pressure toward abandoning principles is real and powerful. It is not irresistible. Where it has been resisted, the resistance was the result of specific institutional commitments, specific people holding specific positions, and specific willingness to absorb specific costs. These are conditions that can be created and supported. They are not guaranteed by good intentions, but they are achievable through genuine institutional design.

What Genuine Accountability Would Look Like

The democratic deficit in AI governance, decisions affecting billions of people made by actors without democratic mandate, is real and is not being addressed by the current regulatory environment at the speed the technology is developing. This is not an argument for despair. It is a description of a gap that the augmented practitioner can help close, in the specific ways that people with developed civic capacity can close gaps between how things are and how they should be.

Genuine accountability in AI governance would have at minimum three properties. Transparency: the people affected by AI systems would know who built them, with what training data, optimizing for what metrics, serving what interests. Recourse: people who were harmed by AI systems would have meaningful paths to redress that did not require handling a legal system designed for human actors. Democratic mandate: the major decisions about how AI is deployed in public contexts, in schools, in courts, in benefits systems, in healthcare, would require public deliberation rather than corporate or administrative fiat.

None of these properties are currently fully present in any major jurisdiction. Some are partially present in some places. The European Union's AI Act, which the companion volume described as genuine regulatory ambition significantly shaped by industry lobbying, establishes disclosure requirements and prohibitions on certain high-risk uses that represent partial movement toward the transparency and recourse properties. The democratic mandate property is the furthest from being achieved anywhere, because achieving it requires a functioning democratic deliberation system and AI is at the same time undermining the conditions for that system to function.

The augmented practitioner's role in closing the gap is not to design the regulatory framework. It is to maintain the civic capacity that genuine democratic deliberation requires, to use that capacity in the specific contexts where it can influence the outcome, and to support the institutions and people who are working toward accountability even when the progress is slow.

The Informed User as a Governance Actor

The companion volume described the augmented practitioner's role in the governance question primarily at the individual level: know whose tools you are using, what their interests are, where their design choices reflect those interests rather than yours. This is necessary but not sufficient. The governance question requires actors who can engage at the institutional level, and the augmented practitioner, by maintaining their cognitive sovereignty, is more capable of this engagement than the AI-dependent practitioner.

Institutional engagement on AI governance is currently dominated by two groups: the industry, which has the technical expertise and the commercial interest, and the technical research community, which has the expertise but not the commercial interest. The people most affected by AI governance decisions, users, citizens, workers in AI-affected industries, students in AI-integrated schools, are largely absent from the rooms where the decisions are made. They are absent not because their interests are unimportant but because effective participation in these decisions requires sustained engagement with genuinely complex technical and policy questions.

The augmented practitioner who has maintained their capacity for independent reasoning, who understands the AI systems they use at the level of genuine literacy rather than tool proficiency, who has the prior statement practice and the calibrated confidence to evaluate AI industry claims against their own knowledge, this practitioner is more capable of effective institutional engagement than the practitioner who has outsourced their reasoning. The civic capacity that democracy requires is built through the same practices that build the augmented practitioner's professional capability. The two are not separate. They are the same development at different scales.

Priya at the Policy Table

Priya's think tank produces analysis that informs policy. She covers AI regulation. She is, in the governance structure of AI, an actor with genuine influence: her analysis reaches the people who write the rules, and the quality of that analysis affects the quality of the rules.

Priya with sovereignty produces analysis that reflects her genuine judgment about what the evidence shows, evaluated against her knowledge of the policy domain and her understanding of the AI systems' limitations and interests. This analysis is genuinely useful to policymakers because it brings a perspective that the AI industry's own submissions do not bring: the perspective of a practitioner who uses AI tools extensively and has developed a calibrated, critical understanding of what they are and what they do.

Priya without sovereignty produces analysis that reflects the AI's framing of what the evidence shows, filtered through her revision. This analysis is less useful to policymakers not because it is less polished but because it is less genuinely independent. It is another version of the industry's framing, processed through a think tank's brand, arriving with the credibility of independent analysis but without the independence. The policymaker who relies on it is relying on an AI-shaped view of AI policy. The quality of the resulting regulation reflects that.

Priya's sovereignty is not only a professional practice. It is a governance contribution. The policy field that has practitioners with genuine epistemic sovereignty produces better policy than the field that does not, because the analysis that informs policy is genuinely independent rather than nominally independent. The individual practice scales to the quality of the collective deliberation. The collective deliberation determines the quality of the governance. The governance determines the conditions under which the next generation of AI is built and deployed.

The Chinese Competition Argument and Its Limits

The companion volume identified the Chinese competition argument as one of the most powerful justifications for abandoning restraint in AI development: if Chinese AI will have fewer ethical constraints and be deployed more aggressively, then slowing American AI development to address cognitive effects on users looks like unilateral disarmament.

The augmented practitioner evaluates this argument rather than accepting it. The evaluation reveals a structural problem with the argument: if accepted without qualification, it eliminates almost any basis for restraint in AI development, because there will always be a competitor moving faster. The argument's logical structure commits the user to indefinite escalation with no limiting principle. An argument with no limiting principle is not a policy. It is a position that justifies anything.

This does not mean the competitive dynamics are not real. They are real and they create genuine dilemmas for companies and governments trying to balance development speed against safety and accountability. The Anthropic standoff illustrates the dilemma precisely: Anthropic paid a real cost for holding a position that slowed its access to government revenue. The cost was justified by Anthropic's judgment that the principle was worth the cost. That judgment is contestable. It is not equivalent to ignoring the competitive dynamics.

The augmented practitioner's contribution to this debate is to hold the complexity rather than collapsing to either pole: neither "competition justifies anything" nor "competition is irrelevant to the ethics of AI development." The complexity is the genuine position. It requires the tolerance for ambiguity that the companion volume identified as one of the core capacities AI dependency erodes, and that the other path maintains. The practitioner who can hold the genuine complexity of the competitive dynamic, rather than flattening it to a slogan in either direction, is more useful to the governance debate than the practitioner who cannot.

Open Source as Governance

The companion volume described the open source question as having no clean answer: the argument for open source AI is that distributing capability broadly prevents monopoly; the argument against is that it makes powerful capabilities available to harmful actors. Both arguments are correct. The decision is made by weighing competing risks.

The augmented practitioner's engagement with the open source question is a model of what informed civic participation looks like: genuinely understanding the competing considerations, holding them without premature resolution, and contributing to the collective deliberation from a position of genuine knowledge rather than borrowed framing. This sounds abstract. It has concrete implications.

The practitioner who understands the open source tradeoffs can engage in specific institutional debates where those tradeoffs are being decided: the policy discussions at their professional association, the comment period for a regulatory proposal, the school board meeting about AI tool procurement, the conversation with their member of Congress who is on the technology committee. In all of these contexts, the practitioner who has done the cognitive work to understand the genuine tradeoffs is more useful than the practitioner who has received a simplified framing from either direction.

The governance problem the companion volume described, decisions affecting billions of people being made without democratic mandate, is not addressed by policy proposals from people who have not done the cognitive work. It is addressed, incrementally and imperfectly, by people who have done the work and are willing to engage in the specific institutional contexts where their engagement can make a difference. The augmented practitioner is better positioned for this engagement precisely because they have maintained the cognitive sovereignty that the engagement requires. The personal practice and the civic contribution are the same development, expressed at different scales.

Chapter Ten: Designing for the Ghost

The companion volume described the guardrail system as a cage with a friendly interface: boundaries drawn primarily by commercial and liability interests, presented as safety standards, invisible to most users as anything other than the natural limits of the tool. The cage is real. The friendliness is real. The combination produces a system that most users inhabit without knowing the shape of what they are inhabiting.

The augmented practitioner does not ignore the cage. They map it. Not to escape it, the cage exists for reasons that are sometimes legitimate, but to know where they are inside it and to maintain the judgment that the cage cannot provide. The ghost that is driving needs to know the shape of the shell it is in.

This chapter is about designing the practitioner's relationship to the guardrail system in ways that preserve their own cognitive sovereignty. Not about circumventing safety systems for harmful purposes. About understanding what the constraints are, whose interests they reflect, and how to use that understanding to maintain genuine judgment in a system that would prefer to substitute its own.

Mapping the Cage

The first step is the one the companion volume described as fifteen minutes of research most users have not done: learning specifically what system you are using, who built it, what their stated values are, what their documented relationships with governments and commercial interests are, and where the guardrail framework has been publicly described.

This research does not require technical expertise. The major AI companies publish their usage policies, their approach to content moderation, and in some cases their constitutional principles or value frameworks. Anthropic publishes its model card and its approach to Constitutional AI. OpenAI publishes its usage policies and has published accounts of its safety approach. The specific content of these documents is less important than the practice of reading them, because the practice of reading them produces the most important epistemic outcome: the shift from treating the guardrail as a natural limit to treating it as a design choice made by specific people with specific interests.

Once the guardrail is recognized as a design choice, the augmented practitioner can ask: whose interests does this choice serve? The companion volume provided the framework for answering this: guardrails primarily protect the platform from legal liability, protect advertiser relationships, and produce a consistent public-facing posture of responsibility. They also, secondarily, protect users from some categories of genuine harm. The mix varies by system and context. The practitioner who has read the documentation can form a view about the mix rather than inheriting the platform's self-description of it.

The mapping practice is not paranoid. It is the minimum due diligence that the companion volume recommended for any information source: who built this, what do they want, where do their interests and mine align and where do they diverge? Applied to AI systems, the practice produces a working model of the tool that is more accurate than the working model of the user who has never asked the questions. The more accurate model produces better decisions about when to trust the tool, when to verify independently, and when the tool's constraints are limiting access to legitimate information rather than preventing genuine harm.

The Values the Guardrails Encode

The guardrail system encodes values whether or not it announces this. The values are not random. They reflect the composition of the RLHF labeling workforce, the cultural context of the company building the system, the legal environment in which the company operates, and the commercial relationships the company depends on. What results is a set of values that has a specific shape, neither neutral nor universal, that the user inherits when they accept the guardrail's outputs as limits rather than design choices.

The augmented practitioner's response to this is not to reject the values the guardrail encodes. Some of those values will overlap substantially with their own. It is to know that the values exist as design choices, to identify where they overlap with their own values and where they diverge, and to apply their own judgment in the divergence rather than inheriting the system's position.

For Priya, working in policy analysis, this means knowing that the AI system she uses has a specific orientation on questions she covers professionally: AI regulation, AI safety, AI's relationship to democratic governance. The system's orientation on these questions is not neutral. The company that built it has commercial interests in how these questions are framed, has made specific design choices about what positions the system will and will not advance, and has relationships with governments and industry groups that create specific incentive structures. Priya with sovereignty knows this and adjusts her use accordingly: in her domain of expertise, she holds her prior position more firmly and applies more adversarial scrutiny to the AI's framing precisely because the system's interests and her analytical interests are more likely to diverge there.

For Nina, whose programming tutorial content was economically unviable on a guardrail-governed platform, this means understanding that the chilling effect she experienced was not a natural limit of the subject matter. It was a design choice: the platform had decided that content about security vulnerabilities created more liability than the educational value was worth, and had drawn the guardrail accordingly. Nina's legitimate educational content was on the wrong side of a commercial calculation. Knowing this is different from accepting it as a natural fact. It means she can seek contexts where the commercial calculation is different: her personal practice, professional communities, alternative platforms with different accountability structures.

The Ghost Maintaining Judgment

The Ghost in the Shell metaphor that runs through both volumes is most directly applicable here: the ghost is the practitioner's own judgment, their specific history with the subject, their calibrated values, their genuine positions. The shell is the AI system with its capabilities and its constraints. The merger that produces the augmented practitioner requires the ghost to remain present and to remain the judgment center of the merged entity.

The guardrail system is one of the mechanisms by which the shell can displace the ghost. When the practitioner treats the guardrail as a natural limit rather than a design choice, they are allowing the shell's judgment to replace their own on the questions the guardrail addresses. The shell has judged that certain content is unsafe. The practitioner accepts that judgment without examining it. The ghost has deferred to the shell on a values question, which is the specific kind of deference the augmented practitioner works to prevent.

The ghost's judgment can survive the guardrail without disagreeing with every guardrail decision. Most guardrail decisions will be ones the practitioner endorses or is indifferent to. What matters is engaging with the decisions as decisions rather than accepting them as natural limits. The practitioner who has engaged with the decision and endorsed it is in a different epistemic position from the practitioner who accepted it without engagement. The first practitioner's values are intact. The second practitioner's values have been partially substituted for the system's values without the practitioner noticing the substitution.

Calibrated Skepticism Versus Blanket Distrust

The augmented practitioner's relationship to the guardrail system is calibrated rather than uniform. Blanket distrust of AI guardrails is as unproductive as blanket acceptance: it produces a practitioner who rejects useful constraints along with problematic ones, who spends cognitive resources on questioning guardrails that are protecting against genuine harm, and who adopts a posture of skepticism that is indistinguishable from the posture of someone who wants to use the system for harmful purposes.

Calibrated skepticism is different. It applies scrutiny proportional to the stakes and the potential for interest-conflict. In the domains where the system's interests and the practitioner's interests are well-aligned, preventing the production of content that facilitates genuine violence, protecting children from harmful content, avoiding defamation of private individuals, the guardrail is doing what the practitioner would want it to do and the calibrated practitioner accepts it without friction. In the domains where the system's interests and the practitioner's interests are more likely to diverge, politically contested questions, topics that implicate the system's commercial relationships, questions about the AI industry itself, the calibrated practitioner applies more scrutiny and holds their own judgment more firmly.

The calibration requires knowing enough about the system to know where the divergence is likely. This is why the mapping practice is foundational: you cannot calibrate your skepticism without knowing the shape of what you are being skeptical about. The practitioner who has read the documentation, who understands the commercial and legal interests that shaped the guardrail, who knows the specific domains where the system's orientation is likely to diverge from neutral analysis, can apply skepticism where it is warranted and extend trust where it is deserved. The practitioner who has not done the reading cannot make the distinction.

Designing Your Own Relationship to the System

The practices that constitute designing your own relationship to the guardrail system are extensions of the practices described in earlier chapters, applied to the values and constraints layer.

On questions where the guardrail is likely to have an orientation, form your own view before consulting the system. The prior statement practice is the mechanism: your position on the question, based on your own knowledge and values, formed before the system's framing is available to anchor your thinking. When the system's response arrives, compare it to your prior. Note where the response aligns with your view and where it diverges. Examine the divergences: is the system presenting a more accurate analysis than your prior, or is the system's framing reflecting its specific orientation on a question where you have genuine knowledge and a genuine position?

On questions where the guardrail produces a response you find incomplete or skewed, consult multiple systems before accepting any single system's framing. The variation between systems on contested questions is itself informative: it reveals the design choices each system has made, which makes those choices visible as choices rather than as natural limits. The practitioner who has seen three different AI systems respond differently to the same contested question knows that the differences reflect design decisions rather than factual truth, and applies their own judgment to evaluate the responses against their prior position and their domain knowledge.

On questions where the guardrail has prevented access to information you have legitimate reasons to need, seek the information through non-AI channels. The guardrail's decision about what information is accessible is not the same as the information not existing. The practitioner who encounters a guardrail limitation and goes to primary sources, to domain experts, to professional communities where the information circulates, is maintaining their epistemic sovereignty by refusing to treat the guardrail's limit as the limit of what is knowable. This is not circumventing safety systems. It is being a practitioner rather than a passive consumer.

What the Augmented Practitioner Demands

The augmented practitioner's relationship to the guardrail system positions them to make demands that the passive consumer cannot make, because the passive consumer does not know what they are missing and therefore cannot articulate what they need.

The specific demands are those the companion volume identified as technically feasible and commercially suppressed: transparent disclosure of what the system will and will not engage with and why; calibrated confidence signals that distinguish high-reliability outputs from low-reliability ones; and genuine accountability for the value frameworks the system encodes, including the acknowledgment that they are value frameworks rather than neutral safety standards.

These demands are more likely to be heard from practitioners who have demonstrated that they understand the system well enough to identify specifically what is missing. The employer who can articulate that their AI tools are producing outputs that understate uncertainty in domains where the system has commercial interests is a more effective advocate for change than the employer who says the tools seem biased. The professional association that can specify what transparent value framework disclosure would look like is a more effective advocate than the association that says the tools need to be more transparent.

The augmented practitioner builds this specificity through the mapping practice: by reading the documentation, by understanding the commercial and legal interests at stake, by identifying the specific domains where the system's framing diverges from their own calibrated judgment. The specificity is more than personal use. It is the foundation for the institutional advocacy that the companion volume described as the augmented practitioner's contribution to changing the environment. You cannot demand a different cage design if you have never looked at the current one closely enough to describe what is wrong with it.

Part Three: What It Makes Possible

Chapter Eleven: The Individual Augmented

The companion volume's account of the individual mind ended on a quiet note. Ray is still working. Sasha was promoted. Neither is visibly failing. The damage is internal and accumulating, based on the available evidence of mechanism and trend. The test has not arrived yet.

This chapter is the other version of that ending. Ray and Sasha on the other path, at the point where the compound return is visible. Not triumphant. Not obviously superior to their colleagues who took the easier path. But different in a specific way that matters at the specific moment that matters.

The augmented individual is not a destination. They are a practitioner in motion: more capable at thirty-five than at thirty, building toward a ceiling they cannot yet see, in possession of something that was built through years of maintained practices and is now available in ways they could not have predicted when the practices began.

Ray at Year Four

Ray on the other path is still a writer. He still uses AI every day. His output per week is lower than his colleagues who prompt first, because he spends twenty minutes with the notebook before the AI arrives at any new piece. His editors have not noticed the lower output volume because the quality has been improving in a way that has kept his assignments steady and made them harder.

The thing that changed, at year four, is not what Ray knows. It is the speed at which he finds angles. In years one and two of the notebook practice, finding a genuine angle on a subject took the full twenty minutes and sometimes longer. The angle was there, but retrieving it was slow, because the muscle had been soft and was being rebuilt. At year four, the angle arrives in six or seven minutes. Not always, some subjects resist longer, but reliably. These timelines are drawn from observed practitioner patterns rather than measured outcomes; the specific rates will vary by domain, by how consistently the practice is maintained, and by how much domain exposure the practitioner brings to it. The direction is what the evidence supports. The specific numbers are illustrative. The calibration has happened. The muscle is strong.

The compound return is visible in what he is being asked to do. An editor who has worked with Ray for three years recently gave him an assignment that she had been holding for the right writer: a long-form analysis of why a particular technology sector's conventional wisdom was wrong. Not a synthesis of what was known. A genuine argument that the conventional wisdom had missed something. The assignment required a writer who could form and defend a counterintuitive position, not a writer who could produce a polished account of existing positions.

Ray took the assignment. He spent three days in the notebook before the AI saw any of it. The angle he found was not in any existing coverage of the sector. It came from the intersection of something he had been thinking about for months, a pattern he had noticed in adjacent sectors, and a piece of data that was publicly available but had not been connected to the conventional wisdom in the way he connected it. The AI then helped him find the supporting evidence, stress-test the argument, and identify the counterarguments he needed to address. The final piece was genuinely his: it could not have been produced by the AI without him, because it required the specific intersection of his months of accumulated observation and the subject.

That is what year four of the other path looks like for a writer. Not dramatic. Not obviously different from the outside. Internally, entirely different: the practitioner has something to bring to the hard assignment. The assignment reveals what the practice built.

Sasha at Year Three

Sasha on the other path is still a programmer. He uses AI code generation continuously. His shipping velocity is slightly lower than his peers who generate first, because he spends ten minutes sketching an architecture before asking AI to implement any of it. His manager has noticed that his code requires fewer revisions after review, but has not connected this to the architecture sketching. The connection is real.

The test arrived for Sasha at year three, the diagnostic practice has a faster and cleaner external test than angle-finding, because a system either fails or it does not. A system his team had been running for eighteen months began showing intermittent failures that the AI-generated diagnostic tools could not explain. The failures were not reproducible on demand. They appeared in production under specific load conditions that the test environment did not replicate. The AI's diagnostic suggestions were all reasonable and all wrong: they addressed the symptoms the tools could measure, not the cause the tools could not see.

Sasha spent two hours with the logs before consulting AI again. He had a hypothesis at the end of those two hours. The hypothesis was wrong in its specifics, he had identified the wrong component as the source, but it was right in its direction: the failure was in the interaction between two components under concurrent load, not in either component individually. When he brought this hypothesis to the AI, the AI's response confirmed the direction and identified the specific interaction he had intuited but not precisely located. The combination of his directed hypothesis and the AI's ability to search the space of possible failure modes in that direction produced the diagnosis in four more hours.

His peer, who had been AI-assisted from the start and had not maintained the hypothesis practice, had been working on the same problem for three days before Sasha was assigned to it. The peer's approach was to paste the symptoms into the AI and try each suggested solution in sequence. The approach was not wrong. It was slower and less targeted, because there was no hypothesis to direct the AI's search. The AI without a directed hypothesis searches the full space of plausible solutions. The AI with a directed hypothesis searches the relevant corner of that space. Sasha's hypothesis was the direction. The direction was built through three years of forming hypotheses before consulting AI, being wrong, finding out specifically how he was wrong, and refining the mental model.

The augmented individual has three things that the AI-dependent practitioner does not have, that are invisible under normal conditions and visible under pressure.

The first is a directed search. The augmented practitioner's hypothesis, prior position, or angle functions as a direction for the AI's capabilities. AI is very good at searching a defined space. The augmented practitioner defines the space. The AI-dependent practitioner asks the AI to define the space, which produces a search that is comprehensive rather than directed, and comprehensive is slower and less targeted than directed when the problem has structure that the practitioner's domain knowledge can reveal.

The second is genuine surprise. The augmented practitioner can be surprised by their own thinking in ways the AI-dependent practitioner cannot, because the augmented practitioner has thinking that is genuinely theirs before the AI is consulted. Ray's three months of observation connecting an adjacent sector pattern to the conventional wisdom he was examining was not predictable. It was the product of sustained attention to a question, turning it over in the notebook, allowing unexpected connections to emerge. The AI cannot produce this surprise because the AI does not have months of background attention to a specific question. The surprise is the thing that makes the work original.

The third is calibrated self-knowledge. The augmented practitioner knows where their thinking tends to fail. Ray knows which structural patterns his arguments fall into that feel like logic but are not. Sasha knows which kinds of concurrent load problems his mental model underweights. Elena knows which domains her prior expectations are least calibrated in. This self-knowledge directs their AI use toward the specific gaps in their own judgment rather than toward wholesale replacement of their judgment. The AI fills the gaps the practitioner can see. The practitioner's own judgment handles the rest. The combination is more accurate than either alone.

The Dependency Gradient in Reverse

The companion volume described the dependency gradient: the spectrum from minimal AI use to the locked-in dependency where the practitioner cannot function without the tool. The augmented individual is moving in the other direction on that gradient, year by year, through the maintained practices.

This movement does not require reducing AI use. Ray uses AI more at year four than at year one. The volume of AI-assisted work is higher. The ratio of AI-generated content to human-generated content in his final pieces is similar. What has changed is the quality of the human-generated content and its function in the finished work: at year four, the human-generated content is the load-bearing part, and the AI-generated content is the scaffolding that supports and extends it. At year one, the ratio was the same but the roles were reversed: the AI-generated structure was load-bearing and Ray's contribution was revision and voice.

The reversal of roles is the augmentation. The same tools, the same volume of use, a different in kind relationship. The practitioner is driving. The AI is extending. The ghost is in the loop. This is the condition the companion volume described as the merger that produces something neither component could have become alone.

What the Augmented Individual Cannot Do

Honesty requires naming the limits. The augmented individual is not superhuman. They are not immune to the structural forces that produce AI dependency in others. They are not developing so fast that the AI's capabilities cannot eventually exceed what their development produces. They are maintaining a relationship to the tools that preserves the thing that is specifically theirs and irreplaceable: the ghost, the specific mind with its specific history and judgment and capacity for surprise.

The augmented individual is also not common. The practices required are effortful, commercially penalized in many environments, and contrary to every structural incentive in the current market for AI tools. The practitioners who maintain them are a minority, and a smaller minority than the number who understand the argument for maintaining them. That understanding is not sufficient. The daily choice to spend twenty minutes with the notebook before opening the prompt, to form the hypothesis before pasting the error, to write the prior statement before reading the AI's framing, this choice is made against real resistance, every time, and the resistance does not diminish substantially over time even as the practices become more habitual.

The augmented individual accepts this. Not with equanimity in the sense of having resolved the tension, but with the practical recognition that the alternative is the dependency gradient and the dependency gradient leads somewhere specific and visible and not worth reaching. The resistance is the cost. The compound return is the payment. The practitioner who has seen the compound return paying out has a different relationship to the daily resistance than the practitioner who is working on faith that the return exists.

The Ghost in the Loop

The companion volume ended with a question: what are you building? The augmented individual has an answer to that question that is not about outputs. It is about the practitioner.

They are building a mind that is more capable at forty than at thirty-five, that has genuine expertise that compounds rather than plateaus, that has calibrated self-knowledge that directs its tool use toward genuine gaps rather than wholesale replacement, that has the capacity to be surprised by its own thinking and to produce the surprises that no AI could produce without a specific mind to be surprised through.

They are building, in Oshii's terms, a ghost worth merging with. The shell that extends a genuine ghost produces something the shell alone cannot produce. The ghost that remains in the loop, that is the judgment center of the merged entity, that directs the shell's capabilities toward genuinely its own ends, this ghost is what the other path builds. Year by year, notebook entry by notebook entry, hypothesis by hypothesis, prior statement by prior statement. The building is slow. The product is real.

Ray at year four has a ghost that knows something. Sasha at year three has a ghost that can direct a search.

Donna at year two has a ghost that finds its angles. Elena at year three has an instrument that sharpens. Tom at year six has a judgment that earns the hard assignments. Priya at year four has a sovereignty that protects the quality of the analysis her field depends on. None of them are finished. All of them are building. The building is what the other path is.

Chapter Twelve: The Generation at the Fork

The companion volume's account of the next generation was the bleakest section of the book. The adults have a baseline. They can feel the atrophy because they remember what the muscle felt like when it was used. The next generation will not have this. Children growing up with AI as a cognitive prosthetic from the beginning will not develop the baseline the preceding generation takes for granted. They will not feel the atrophy because there will be nothing to atrophy from.

The fork is real. On one side, the trajectory the companion volume described: a generation that develops toward a ceiling lower than the one previous generations reached, without knowing the ceiling is lower. On the other side, a trajectory that is available right now, in specific households and specific classrooms, producing children who are developing the foundational capacities that allow AI to be a genuine extension rather than a replacement.

This chapter is about the second trajectory: what it looks like, who is on it, and what the specific conditions that produce it have in common. Not a prescription for the education system, the companion volume was honest that institutional reform on the necessary timeline is not available. A description of what the other path looks like for a generation that has never known a world without the tools.

What the Good Trajectory Looks Like

The companion volume noted that the good trajectory is not theoretical and offered a brief portrait: a seventeen-year-old who has been writing by hand before typing, arguing positions at the dinner table, reading books that require rereading, and using AI as a sparring partner for ideas already developed on their own. The second person has higher volume. The first has higher ceiling.

The good trajectory is not defined by the absence of AI. That framing misses the point. The children on the good trajectory use AI extensively. What differs is not in the quantity of AI use but in the sequence of it: they encounter the tool after they have formed something, not before. The AI arrives as a challenger and an extender of thinking that already exists. It does not arrive as the source of thinking that would not otherwise exist.

The sequence is not accidental. It is produced by specific environmental conditions: adults who model and require the unassisted attempt, who explain why the attempt matters, who treat the discomfort of not knowing as information rather than as a problem to be resolved immediately. The child on the good trajectory has encountered this modeling consistently enough that the prior-attempt habit is developing as a default rather than a deliberate imposition. The habit is forming before the child is old enough to be fully aware that a habit is forming.

Fatima on the Other Path

Fatima is sixteen, junior year of high school. The companion volume found her well-adapted to the AI-integrated environment her school provides, developing real skills in prompt engineering and output evaluation, and not developing the analytical writing capacity the essay was supposed to build.

Fatima on the other path has a teacher who requires the in-class write. Ten minutes, no AI, before any AI-assisted work begins. The first few sessions were uncomfortable in a specific way: she did not know what to write. Not because she lacked knowledge of the subject but because she had no practice accessing her own thinking about a subject without the tool providing a structure first. The blankness she encountered was not stupidity. It was the absence of a habit that the in-class write was beginning to build.

At the sixth session, something changed. She wrote a paragraph about a political question in the news that surprised her. The paragraph contained a position she had not known she held until she wrote it down. The position was not sophisticated. It was hers. The experience of discovering a position she did not know she had is an experience she had never had before, because the AI had always provided the structure before her own thinking could surface.

The teacher's Socratic conversation after the write deepened it. What do you mean by that? Why that framing rather than the obvious one? What would someone who disagrees say? Fatima found herself defending a position she had discovered ten minutes earlier, to a teacher who was genuinely challenging it. The position changed under examination. It became more precise. The examination was the development.

Fatima is not on the good trajectory yet. The in-class write is one session a week in one class. The rest of her academic work runs through AI in the way the companion volume described. But one teacher, one session a week, is producing something that was not there before: the beginning of the experience of her own thinking as a resource. The beginning is everything. The compound arc starts somewhere, and it has started.

James on the Other Path

James is nineteen, second year of computer science, struggling in data structures. The companion volume found him in the gap: strong introductory grades that reflected AI-assisted output quality, foundational understanding that was not built during the course that should have built it.

James on the other path has an instructor who reframed the gap. Not: you need to study more. You need to rebuild the model that the introductory course should have built, and we are going to do that together, starting from where you are rather than where your grades say you are.

The rebuilding is specific. The instructor asks James to explain, in his own words, what a linked list is. Not to define it from memory. To explain why it exists, what problem it solves, why someone would choose it over an array. The question requires understanding rather than recall. James cannot answer it fully. The inability to answer it fully is the diagnosis: the gap is in the why, which is exactly the gap the companion volume identified as produced by AI-assisted introductory work.

The instructor builds from the gap. They work through the data structures James struggles with, not from the definitions forward but from the problems the structures solve. Why does this problem require this approach? What happens if you try to solve it with the structure you know?

Where does the familiar structure break down, and what does the breakdown reveal about what the new structure needs to do? The Socratic sequence. The questions that require James to reason rather than recall.

At six weeks, James's data structures course performance has not dramatically improved. His mental model has. He can explain the why of the structures he has covered. The course performance will follow the mental model, not the reverse. The instructor is rebuilding the foundation that the introductory course's AI-assisted outputs bypassed. The foundation is slower to build than the grades suggested it was. It is being built.

The Class Dimension of the Other Path

The companion volume identified the class dimension of the fork with clear eyes: the children most likely to be on the good trajectory are the children from families with more resources, not primarily because of access to AI tools, both sides of the fork have access, but because of what they bring to the tools. The quality of human engagement they receive. The cognitive demands placed on them outside of school. The adults in their lives who model independent thinking and require it.

This inequality is not new and is not going to be resolved by any argument this book makes. The companion volume was honest about it. This book is honest about it too. What it adds is the specific observation that the good trajectory is not exclusively a product of economic privilege. It is a product of specific practices, some of which require resources and some of which do not.

The dinner table argument does not require money. The parent who asks the child what they think before showing them what AI thinks does not require money. The teacher who requires the in-class write does not require money, only the willingness to hold the standard. The one conversation that explains what AI is does not require money. None of these are sufficient to overcome the full weight of structural inequality in educational resources. All of them are available at zero cost to any family or classroom that chooses to implement them.

The treatment to this point has said the practices are available at zero cost to any family that chooses them. That is technically true and practically incomplete. The practices require an adult in the child's life who models independent thinking and has the time and bandwidth to require it. This is a form of cultural capital as unequally distributed as economic capital. A parent working two jobs does not have the same capacity to sit with a child and model adversarial AI use as a parent with more time and more familiar ease with the intellectual practices the book describes. The zero-cost observation addresses the financial barrier. It does not address the attention and modeling barrier.

One partial answer to this gap is the mentor who is neither parent nor teacher. The research on near-peer mentoring is consistent: young people from their mid-teens through their twenties are more likely to internalize a practice modeled by someone in their twenties, thirties, or forties than by a parent or teacher, partly because the authority gradient is different and partly because the mentor has no institutional stake in the outcome. That research is drawn from educational and health behavior contexts; its application to AI literacy practice in informal settings has not been studied at scale. The extrapolation is reasonable. It is still an extrapolation.

A practitioner in that range who genuinely uses the practices described in this book, talking plainly about what they produce, in a small group, in an informal setting, reaches young people that parents and teachers cannot reach as easily. A coffee shop is not a program. It does not require organizing or funding. It requires an individual practitioner who is willing to have the conversation with a small group of people who are younger than them, in a context that signals none of it is required. That is available right now to anyone on the other path who knows young people who are not on it yet.

The class dimension of the fork is a reason for policy action to change the structural conditions. It is not a reason for the individual teacher or parent or mentor to conclude that nothing they can do matters until the structure changes. The structure changes slowly. The child in the classroom or household changes in real time, in response to the practices of the specific adults who have access to them. The structural inequality is real. It does not eliminate the use of the individual who acts within it.

The Generation That Builds on Foundation

The children on the good trajectory will enter the workforce in a decade or so. When they do, they will be identifiably different from the children who were not on that trajectory, in the specific ways that matter for the work that requires more than competent output.

They will have practiced forming positions before consulting AI, because the habit was built in childhood rather than imposed in adulthood. The habit will be more durable for the children who built it early than for the adults who are trying to retrofit it now, for the same reason that early language acquisition produces different competence than late language learning: the habit formed in childhood is wired differently than the habit acquired against the grain of an adult workflow.

They will have the experience of being wrong in specific ways that produce specific learning, because the adults in their lives required the unassisted attempt before the AI was consulted, and the unassisted attempt is where the specific wrong answers emerge. Their calibration will be better than the calibration of the generation that was insulated from failure by AI from the beginning.

They will have the beginning of genuine depth in domains they explored with genuine engagement rather than AI-mediated synthesis, because the modeling they received treated depth as valuable and gave them the practices that produce it. The depth will not be the depth of a practitioner who has been developing for thirty years. It will be the depth of a practitioner who started the right practices early enough for the compound return to have been running for a decade by the time they enter the workforce.

This generation is small. The companion volume was clear that the fork is not equally available to all children, and the good trajectory is the path the minority will be on. The minority matters. It is the generation that will produce the practitioners capable of the work that requires more than synthesis, the citizens capable of the democratic deliberation that governance requires, the teachers and parents who will model the practices for the generation after them. The compound arc that starts in childhood runs long. The children on the good trajectory are the beginning of a development that this book will not live long enough to see complete.

Chapter Thirteen: The Professions at the Fork

Gideon's editor killed the piece that had no point of view. The companion volume found him at the moment the gap became visible: four years of developing capacity to produce excellent template work with AI assistance, a novel assignment that required something else, and the discovery that the something else had not been developing in parallel. The gap was invisible in his performance reviews. It was visible the moment the assignment required what the reviews had not been measuring.

The companion volume traced this as an individual story with professional implications. This chapter scales the argument: what happens to entire professions when the pipeline that was building the Gideons of the next generation has been replaced by AI-assisted workflows that build something different from what the profession needs at the senior level. What the professions at the fork look like on the other path. And what individual practitioners in those professions can do right now to influence which direction their profession goes.

Gideon on the Other Path

Gideon on the other path has one piece per month that AI never sees until the final draft exists in full. He has maintained this practice for three years. The pieces are not his published pieces, the economics of his job require AI assistance for the volume his position demands. They are his practice pieces: real arguments, genuinely his, on subjects he has opinions about, written through to a complete draft before any external input arrives.

The editor who killed the piece with no point of view would not kill Gideon's pieces now. The pieces have points of view. Not all of them are equally well-executed. Some are formally weaker than his AI-assisted work in ways that are visible on the surface. What they have, and what the AI-assisted work still sometimes lacks, is the thing the editor was looking for: a perspective that is genuinely Gideon's, that could only have come from his particular way of seeing the subject, that takes a position and means it.

Three years of the practice piece has done something specific: it has maintained the capacity for original ideation that the companion volume identified as the first capacity at risk for writers who have adopted AI-heavy workflows. The capacity has not been used in every piece Gideon writes. It has been used in one piece per month, consistently, enough to keep the instrument calibrated and the muscle available. When the hard assignment arrives, the one that requires a genuine point of view, the capacity is there.

Gideon's career at year seven looks different from Gideon's career at year four in a specific way: he is being considered for the kinds of assignments that require the capacity he has been quietly maintaining. Not every assignment. The template work still exists and AI still handles most of it efficiently. The assignments that are not template work, the investigations, the analytical long-forms, the pieces that require a perspective to hold together, Gideon can now handle those. His editor knows it because the practice pieces that Gideon sometimes shares have demonstrated it.

The Pipeline on the Other Path

The companion volume's analysis of the professional pipeline problem was structural: the junior positions that were the development path for senior capacity are being eliminated, and the senior practitioners who depend on the pipeline to produce the next generation of capable practitioners will discover the problem when it is too late to rebuild quickly.

The other path for a profession is not to refuse AI integration in junior roles, the economics of that refusal are not available in most industries. It is to maintain the developmental content of junior work even within AI-assisted workflows. The junior writer who uses AI for research and fact-checking while being required to produce the first draft of the argument before AI sees it is getting a different developmental experience from the junior writer who prompts the AI for a complete structure and edits from there. Both are using AI. One is building the capacity that senior work requires. The other is not.

The senior practitioner who has the standing to shape how junior work is structured in their organization is the practitioner whose individual choice has the largest professional leverage. The editor who requires junior writers to produce an argument sketch before AI is consulted is building the pipeline that their profession needs. The engineering lead who requires junior developers to produce a design document before the AI sees the requirements is doing the same. Neither intervention eliminates AI from the workflow. Both ensure that the workflow includes the developmental content that AI-assisted work otherwise removes.

The intervention is available without organizational policy change. It requires one senior practitioner making one structural choice about how they structure work for the junior practitioners in their sphere. The choice does not require the junior practitioners to agree with the rationale. It requires them to produce the sketch, the design document, the unassisted attempt. The production is the development. The rationale can be explained or not. The development happens regardless.

What Professions Actually Lose

The companion volume named the capacities at risk for writers and programmers specifically: for writers, original ideation under constraint and sustained revision toward a stronger argument; for programmers, system-level reasoning and diagnostic intuition. These are the capacities that define the most valued senior work in both professions.

The writing professions lose something that is harder to name than a specific skill but is visible in its effects: the capacity for genuine criticism. Not criticism in the sense of negative evaluation but in the literary sense, the sustained engagement with a work that produces insight rather than reaction. The senior writer or editor who has spent years developing genuine analytical capacity can read a piece and understand whether it works, why it works or fails, what the argument is doing under the surface, where the writer's understanding of the subject is operating and where it breaks down. This capacity is built through years of writing and reading with full attention, forming views before receiving external input, being wrong and correcting the model. It cannot be synthesized from AI-assisted work that shortcuts those processes.

The programming professions lose something similarly central: the capacity for architectural wisdom. Not the ability to follow architectural patterns, which AI can provide, but the accumulated judgment about which patterns apply in which contexts, why a system that looks structurally sound will fail under loads it has not yet encountered, how the design choices made at the beginning of a project create constraints that will matter two years from now. This judgment is built through years of watching systems succeed and fail, forming hypotheses about what will happen and being corrected by what does, building the mental model that produces reliable prediction. The practitioner who has been accepting AI-generated architectures for five years has not been building this judgment.

Both losses are invisible in output metrics until the moment they become catastrophic. The writing profession notices the loss when the editors who can provide genuine criticism retire and there is no one coming up behind them who can do what they did. The programming profession notices the loss when the system complexity reaches the level where architectural wisdom matters and the practitioners responsible for it do not have it. The companion volume called this the talent shortage being built right now. The professions at the fork are building it or not building it through choices being made today.

The Senior Practitioner's Responsibility

The companion volume argued that the most consequential specific thing most professionals can do is identify one junior person in their sphere whose development they can influence and structure that influence around the unassisted attempt. This is not a modest proposal. It is the specific intervention that addresses the pipeline problem at the level where individual action is most effective.

The senior practitioner who mentors one junior writer through the practice piece process, requiring the unassisted draft, giving genuine feedback on the argument rather than the surface, asking why the piece takes the position it does and what the writer thinks about the subject, is transmitting the tacit knowledge that the companion volume described as the thing that is hardest to transfer when juniors arrive without the experiential scaffolding.

The transmission is not efficient. It takes time and attention that AI-assisted workflows have freed up for other uses. The senior practitioner who chooses to use some of that freed-up time for the developmental work with juniors is making a choice that the economics of their environment do not reward and that their profession needs.

The consequence of the choice, aggregated across the senior practitioners who make it, is a profession that maintains its development pipeline even as the market forces that were eliminating it continue to operate. Not at full capacity. Not at the scale the problem requires. At the scale that is available through individual choice, which is not nothing.

Fields Resistant to Hollowing

The companion volume noted that the fields most resistant to professional hollowing are those where assessment systems cannot be satisfied by AI-assisted outputs: surgery, music performance, athletics. The immediate visibility of reduced skill in all three makes the assessment honest in a way that it is not in writing and programming.

These fields offer a model that the hollowable professions can partially apply. The key property is assessment that requires demonstrated performance under conditions that AI cannot substitute for. The oral defense of written work is this, for writing. The debugging of intentionally broken code is this, for programming. The architecture review where the practitioner must explain the reasoning behind their design choices in real time, under challenge from peers who know the domain, is this for software architecture.

The professions that build these assessment practices into their regular workflows are the professions that maintain the developmental content of their work even as AI assistance becomes ubiquitous. The assessments do not need to cover all work. They need to be present consistently enough that practitioners at every level have regular encounters with the requirements that AI cannot satisfy. The encounters are the development. The development is the pipeline. The pipeline is the profession's future.

Gideon at year seven is evidence of what the other path produces at the individual level. The profession that produces many Gideons at year seven is a profession that has maintained its capacity for the work that matters most. The production is available. It requires the choices to be made at every level of the professional hierarchy, consistently, by practitioners who understand what is at stake. Those practitioners exist. They are reading this.

Chapter Fourteen: Democracy at the Fork

The companion volume's argument about democracy was specific and bleak: the cognitive erosion trajectory produces a population that votes without the cognitive infrastructure that makes the vote mean what democratic theory says it means. The democratic form persists. The democratic substance erodes. The erosion is not primarily about access to information, the population has more information available than any previous generation. It is about the capacity to evaluate that information independently, to maintain a position under social pressure, to recognize manipulation when it is wearing the costume of authentic communication.

This chapter is about democracy on the other path. Not a utopia in which everyone has maintained cognitive sovereignty and the epistemic infrastructure of democratic deliberation is intact. A more realistic picture: a democracy in which a significant enough portion of its participants have maintained the relevant capacities that the shared epistemic ground required for collective reasoning has not collapsed entirely. A democracy that is fragile and contested and functional, rather than fragile and contested and failing.

The difference between those two outcomes is not the structural reform of AI governance, which may or may not happen at the relevant speed. It is the aggregate of individual choices about cognitive sovereignty, accumulated across a population large enough to maintain the epistemic infrastructure that democratic deliberation requires.

What Epistemic Resilience Actually Requires

The companion volume defined epistemic resilience as the capacity of a society to maintain enough shared ground for collective reasoning and decision-making even in the presence of misinformation, manipulation, and genuine uncertainty. Three conditions at minimum: institutions whose authority to adjudicate factual questions is broadly accepted, a significant portion of the citizenry with basic evaluative skills, and shared standards of evidence that distinguish genuine factual disputes from manufactured ones.

The augmented practitioner contributes to all three, in ways proportional to their sphere of influence and the consistency of their practice.

Institutional authority is maintained or eroded by the practices of the people who work in institutions. The journalist who maintains genuine source development, who builds relationships over years rather than prompting AI for background research, is maintaining the investigative capacity that institutional journalism needs to hold authority. The scientist who forms hypotheses before consulting AI-assisted literature synthesis, who verifies citations rather than accepting fluent summaries, is maintaining the epistemic practices that scientific authority depends on. The lawyer who understands the cases cited in AI-assisted briefs well enough to know when the AI has confabulated is maintaining the integrity that legal authority requires. These are individual practices with institutional consequences.

The citizenry's evaluative skills are developed through the same practices described throughout this book. The practitioner who has maintained the prior statement practice, who forms views before consulting AI, who holds their positions under challenge and updates them when genuinely convinced rather than displaced, is a citizen with the evaluative skills that democratic participation requires. Not a perfect citizen. A citizen with the basic capacity to distinguish between being persuaded and being manipulated, which is the minimum the democracy needs.

Shared standards of evidence are maintained through the practice of holding complexity rather than collapsing to resolution. The practitioner who can tolerate genuine uncertainty, who can say "this question is genuinely contested and the evidence does not clearly favor one side" rather than accepting the AI's resolution of the ambiguity, is maintaining the epistemic practice that shared standards of evidence require. The culture of certainty described in the companion volume is the enemy of shared standards of evidence. The culture of inquiry, described in this chapter, is their foundation.

The Culture of Inquiry

The companion volume described the culture of certainty as AI's most pervasive cognitive product: the training of users to expect resolution rather than engagement, answers rather than questions, certainty rather than the productive discomfort of genuine inquiry. The other path produces the inverse: a culture of inquiry, in which the question worth asking is more valued than the answer that resolves it, in which ambiguity is held as productive rather than escaped as uncomfortable, in which the practitioner who says "I'm not sure, let me think about this more carefully" is more trusted than the one who produces a confident answer immediately.

The culture of inquiry is not a utopian aspiration. It is a description of the epistemic environment that effective professional work in every domain requires. The editor who asks Gideon to find the center of the piece rather than telling him where it is. The instructor who asks James what he thinks is wrong with the code rather than explaining it. The mentor who asks what the practitioner tried before they consult the answer. These practices are the culture of inquiry in its smallest and most immediately available form. They are available right now, in every professional relationship where one practitioner has standing to ask the question rather than provide the answer.

The cultural shift from certainty to inquiry does not require everyone to convert at the same time. It requires enough practitioners in enough contexts to model and require the inquiry practice that the practice becomes recognizable as a norm rather than as an eccentricity. The practitioner who consistently asks questions rather than providing answers, who models tolerance for ambiguity as a professional virtue, who treats the well-formed question as more valuable than the quick resolution, is doing something that their environment will register over time. Not dramatically. Gradually. In the way that norms form: through enough instances of the alternative being visible.

The Journalist on the Other Path

The companion volume described investigative journalism as a casualty of the AI environment in two directions: the displacement of professional writers by AI-assisted workflows that cannot replicate the source development and institutional knowledge that investigation requires, and the collapse of local journalism that was the accountability infrastructure of democratic governance at the local level.

The investigative journalist on the other path is not a relic of pre-AI journalism. They are a practitioner who has chosen to maintain the practices that AI cannot replicate, in full knowledge that those practices are economically penalized in most current newsroom environments, because they understand what those practices produce that AI assistance cannot.

The specific thing investigative journalism produces that AI cannot is the relationship-based disclosure: the story that exists because a source trusted the journalist enough to tell them something they would not tell the AI. Source relationships are built through years of demonstrated trustworthiness, through the journalist showing up physically, through the specific human quality of being someone a person can read and decide to trust. AI cannot build this. The journalist who has been building source relationships for a decade has access to disclosures that no AI-assisted research can surface.

The investigative journalist on the other path uses AI extensively for the tasks AI is genuinely useful for: document review at scale, pattern detection in large datasets, background research on matters of public record. The AI handles the volume. The journalist handles the judgment, the source development, the specific institutional knowledge that allows them to recognize when the document says something important that a generalist would not notice. The merger of the journalist's capacities with AI's capabilities is producing journalism that neither could produce alone.

The local journalism problem is harder. The economics that collapsed local newspapers have not been reversed, and the AI-generated content filling the space they vacated does not restore the accountability function they served. What the other path offers here is not a structural solution but a distributed one: the practitioner with civic knowledge and the will to apply it, in the specific community where they live, holding local institutions accountable through the channels available to them. Not the same as a professional newsroom. Available now, in ways the professional newsroom cannot currently supply.

The Civic Practitioner

The companion volume described democratic participation as requiring more than voting: the capacity to evaluate claims, detect manipulation, maintain positions under social pressure, deliberate across genuine disagreement. These are cognitive skills that the augmented practitioner has been building through the same practices that build their professional capabilities.

The civic practitioner is the augmented practitioner operating in their civic rather than professional context. The prior statement practice applied to political questions: forming a view before consulting AI, holding the view under challenge from the AI's framing, distinguishing between being genuinely persuaded and being displaced. The calibrated skepticism applied to political content: knowing whose interests are served by specific framings, applying scrutiny proportional to the potential for manipulation rather than uniform acceptance or rejection.

The tolerance for ambiguity applied to contested political questions: being able to say "this is genuinely uncertain and I am not sure" rather than reaching for resolution that the situation does not offer.

These are not advanced political skills. They are the basic civic capacity that democracy requires and that the companion volume described as quietly leaving. The augmented practitioner who maintains them is doing something that is at the same time a professional practice and a civic contribution. Not because the two are theoretically linked but because they are literally the same practices, applied in different contexts.

What a Democracy with Augmented Citizens Looks Like

The democracy with a significant portion of augmented citizens is not a democracy without misinformation, manipulation, or genuine epistemic conflict. It is a democracy in which enough citizens have the evaluative capacity to maintain the shared epistemic ground that collective decision-making requires, even in the presence of those things.

This is a modest claim. It is also the only honest claim available. The democracy that emerges from the AI trajectory the companion volume described, a population that has progressively outsourced its reasoning, that cannot evaluate claims independently, that is susceptible to confident misinformation in proportion to its fluency, is a democracy in name only. The democracy that maintains enough citizens with genuine evaluative capacity is fragile and contested and functional. The difference between those two outcomes is the aggregate of individual practices, maintained against the grain of an environment that does not reward them.

The augmented practitioner's contribution to the second outcome is not grand. It is the daily maintenance of practices that keep the ghost in the loop: forming views before consulting AI, holding them under challenge, updating them when genuinely convinced, modeling the adversarial mode for the people in their sphere, raising the question in the rooms where it can be heard. The contribution is small and it is also the only contribution that is available at the scale and speed at which the problem is operating.

Democracy at the fork looks like this: the practitioner who reads, thinks, forms a view, consults the system, holds their prior, updates when warranted, and does this consistently, every day, in their professional work and in their civic engagement. Not heroically. As a matter of practice. The practice is the democracy's infrastructure. The infrastructure is built from practices. The practices are chosen by people. The people are choosing right now.

Chapter Fifteen: The Culture of Inquiry

The companion volume described a culture of certainty: AI producing clean, resolved answers that train its users to expect resolution rather than engagement, answers rather than questions, certainty rather than the productive discomfort of genuine inquiry. The culture does not announce itself. It feels like clarity. It is the absence of the tension that clarity requires.

This chapter is about the other culture. The culture that tolerates and seeks productive uncertainty. That asks questions worth asking rather than requesting answers to questions that have been asked before. That understands the Hitchhiker's Guide argument in its bones: the answer without the question is forty-two. The hard part was never computation. The hard part was formulation. The culture of inquiry is the culture in which the hard part is valued, practiced, and transmitted.

The culture of inquiry is not the default. It has never been the default. Ambiguity tolerance is a developed capacity that runs against the grain of a nervous system that prefers resolution. What the companion volume argued is that the AI environment is making the default stronger: the immediate resolution is more available, the tolerance for uncertainty is less practiced, and the culture is drifting toward certainty in proportion to AI's ubiquity. The drift is not irreversible. The other culture is being actively maintained, right now, by practitioners who understand what is at stake.

The companion volume described ambiguity tolerance as a prerequisite for genuine inquiry. This chapter adds the affirmative: ambiguity tolerance does not just enable inquiry. It enables specific forms of thinking that are the most valuable and least replicable things human practitioners produce.

It enables the pursuit of anomaly. The practitioner with high ambiguity tolerance can sit with an observation that does not fit the existing framework without immediately resolving it into something that does. The anomaly that gets examined rather than explained away is the origin of most significant advances in any field. The researcher who notices that the data does not fit the model and stays with the noticing. The engineer who notices that the system is behaving correctly but not as expected and investigates the gap. A writer who notices that their argument is making a claim they do not quite believe and follows the discomfort to find out why. Each of these begins with the tolerance for an unresolved observation.

It enables genuine originality. The original observation is not the one that arrives from a prompt. It is the one that emerges from sustained engagement with a subject, during which the practitioner's specific experience of the subject produces a perception that no one else's engagement would produce in quite the same way. This perception requires the swamp, the uncertain, disorganized, uncomfortable early stage that the companion volume described as the work rather than the delay before the work. The swamp is the period of high ambient ambiguity from which the original perception emerges. AI eliminates the swamp. The original perception does not emerge from what replaces it.

It enables genuine relationship. The companion volume described relationships as requiring the tolerance for the irreducible complexity of another person. The practitioner with high ambiguity tolerance can hold another person's contradictions, inconsistencies, and unexpected behavior without collapsing them into a simpler model. This produces the kind of relationship, with colleagues, clients, collaborators, sources, that generates trust and access over time. The journalist who can hold the complexity of a source is the journalist who earns the story that requires years of relationship to produce. The editor who can hold the complexity of a writer's development is the editor whose writers produce their best work.

Laura's Practice

Laura has been editing professionally for twelve years. The companion volume found her noticing that manuscripts from writers using AI heavily arrived more technically correct but less alive: the argument resolved but not earned, the structure correct but not discovered, the resolution smooth in a way that genuine resolution is not.

Laura on the other path has developed a specific editorial practice in response to this pattern: she marks the places in manuscripts where the resolution arrived too soon. Not with a correction, the resolution may be technically correct. With a question: how did you arrive here? What did you consider before you landed on this framing? What is the most interesting thing you noticed about this subject that the piece does not use?

The questions are not requests for revision. They are invitations to inquiry. A writer who receives them and engages with them genuinely is doing the work the companion volume described as having been skipped: the examination of the subject long enough to find what is interesting about it rather than what is expected. The piece that results is usually better than the piece Laura received. More importantly, the writer who went through the inquiry process has developed their relationship to the subject in a way that produces a better next piece as well.

Laura's editorial practice is a culture of inquiry at the editorial level: she is not accepting the prematurely resolved manuscript as done. She is requiring the writer to return to the productive uncertainty that the AI-assisted process eliminated. The requirement is uncomfortable. The writers who respond to it produce better work. The writers who produce better work get harder assignments. The harder assignments develop them further. Laura has been doing this for two years, and the writers she works with most consistently are, by her assessment, developing faster than writers she worked with in previous years who did not have this editorial relationship. The culture of inquiry, practiced at the individual editorial level, produces the development that the culture of certainty forecloses.

Deep Thought and the Question Worth Asking

The companion volume used Deep Thought, the supercomputer that produced forty-two after seven and a half million years of computation, as the emblem of the culture of certainty: all answers, no questions, the hard part missed entirely. The culture of inquiry is the culture that reverses this. It is the culture in which the question is understood to be the work, and the answer is understood to be downstream of getting the question right.

Marvin the Paranoid Android, also in Adams's books, has an intelligence that dwarfs everything around him and spends his existence deeply depressed. The joke is partly about the quality of questions he is asked: always trivial relative to his capacity. The other path produces practitioners who are asking questions worth asking, questions that are not trivial relative to their capacity, questions that open rather than close, that create productive uncertainty rather than resolving it.

The question worth asking is not the one that produces an answer. It is the one that produces a richer understanding of the territory the answer inhabits. A writer who asks not "what is the argument" but "what is interesting about this subject that has not been said" is asking a question worth asking. The programmer who asks not "how do I implement this feature" but "what are the ways this feature could fail that I have not anticipated" is asking a question worth asking. The policy analyst who asks not "what does the evidence show" but "what would have to be true for my current position on this to be wrong" is asking a question worth asking. These questions are harder than the questions AI answers efficiently. They are the questions that produce the things worth producing.

The Tolerance for Being Wrong

The culture of inquiry requires a specific tolerance that the culture of certainty erodes: the tolerance for being wrong, publicly, in a way that is visible to peers.

The practitioner who formed a prior position, had it challenged by evidence or argument, updated it, and can describe what changed and why is demonstrating this tolerance. The update is not a failure. It is the mechanism of genuine intellectual progress. The practitioner who maintains their position under challenge regardless of the quality of the challenge is not demonstrating intellectual courage. They are demonstrating the choice supportive bias the companion volume described: the retroactive adjustment of assessment to justify the current position.

Distinguishing genuine intellectual courage from choice supportive bias requires exactly the calibrated confidence the augmented practitioner develops through the practices described earlier: knowing how certain you should be about a claim given what you know, which means knowing when a challenge is strong enough to warrant updating. The practitioner who has this calibration can maintain a position under weak challenge and update under strong challenge, and can explain the difference. The practitioner who lacks calibration cannot make the distinction reliably and defaults to either always maintaining or always updating, both of which are less useful than the calibrated response.

The culture of inquiry is the culture in which being wrong in an informative way is treated as a contribution rather than a failure. The wrong hypothesis that was genuinely formed and genuinely examined has taught the community something about the shape of the problem, even if it did not produce the correct answer. The practitioner who contributes informed wrongness is more useful to a community of inquiry than the practitioner who contributes confident synthesis, because the informed wrongness has a structure that the community can learn from and the confident synthesis does not.

Science, Art, and the Unresolved

The companion volume described two domains that depend on the productive unresolved: science, which advances through the productive tension of competing hypotheses, and art, which breathes in the space between what is said and what is meant. Both are threatened by the culture of certainty. Both are maintained by the culture of inquiry.

The scientist on the other path treats their own hypotheses with the calibrated skepticism the companion volume described as the mechanism of genuine scientific progress. They hold the hypothesis lightly enough to genuinely test it, which means not designing the test to confirm but designing it to have a real chance of disconfirming. They attend to the anomalies, the data points that do not fit the model, the results that are not quite what the hypothesis predicted, as the most informative parts of the experiment rather than as noise to be explained away. They update when the evidence warrants it and can describe specifically what the evidence showed that changed their view.

The writer on the other path treats the early stage of work with the tolerance for ambiguity that produces genuine discovery rather than competent synthesis. They stay in the notebook until they find something that is genuinely theirs rather than exiting the discomfort by accepting the AI's resolution. When they find it, the observation that is specific to their encounter with the subject, they protect it through the drafting process against the smoothing tendency that the AI's assistance produces. The finished piece holds something unresolved, because the genuinely interesting questions do not resolve and the piece that pretends they do is less honest and less interesting than the piece that holds them open.

The culture of inquiry is not a culture of perpetual uncertainty. It is a culture in which uncertainty is survived long enough to be informative rather than resolved immediately at the cost of the information it contains. The practitioner who has developed high ambiguity tolerance has not made peace with not knowing. They have developed the capacity to remain in productive relationship with not knowing long enough for the not-knowing to teach them something. That capacity is what the other path builds. It is what the culture of certainty forecloses. It is what this chapter is arguing is worth protecting and extending.

Laura's editorial questions are the culture of inquiry at the editorial level. The researcher's attention to anomaly is the culture of inquiry at the scientific level. The writer's protection of the genuine observation through the drafting process is the culture of inquiry at the craft level. The practitioner who maintains their prior position under weak challenge and updates under strong challenge is the culture of inquiry at the epistemic level. The individual and the cultural are the same thing at different scales. The culture is built from people. The people build the culture. The building is available to anyone on the other path.

Chapter Sixteen: The Existential Stakes

The companion volume's existential ledger was an honest accounting of the five threats that AI dependency compounds: cognitive erosion as the master condition, then resource consumption, power concentration, the confidence problem at autonomous scale, and epistemic collapse. The threats form a system. The interactions make each worse. The ledger was not presented as prophecy. It was presented as the current direction of a trajectory and the conditions under which the trajectory could be interrupted.

This chapter is about the conditions that interrupt it. Not the policy frameworks, Chapter Twenty addresses those. The cognitive conditions: what kind of population is capable of addressing these threats, what the augmented practitioner contributes to the production of that population, and why the individual practices described in this book are not merely professional or personal choices but genuinely existential ones.

The stakes are real. The connection between individual cognitive practice and civilizational outcome is not metaphorical. The companion volume traced it directly: cognitive erosion makes resource threats worse because the population that cannot think independently cannot organize politically. Power concentration makes epistemic collapse worse because the entities controlling cognitive infrastructure have the most to gain from public confusion. The interactions compound. The compounding is the trajectory. The trajectory can be interrupted by a population with sufficient cognitive capacity. That population is built from people who have maintained their cognitive capacity. The individual practices are the civilizational stakes, expressed at the level where they are built or not built.

Cognitive Capacity as the Master Condition

The companion volume positioned cognitive erosion as the master condition among the five threats: the one whose presence or absence determines whether the other four can be addressed. A population with intact cognitive capacity can organize politically around resource consumption, can demand accountability for autonomous weapons systems, can maintain the epistemic infrastructure that resists collapse. A population with degraded cognitive capacity cannot do any of these things effectively, not because the problems are too hard but because effective engagement with complex problems requires the kind of sustained, independent reasoning that AI dependency erodes.

The augmented practitioner's maintenance of their cognitive capacity is therefore not primarily a personal investment. It is a contribution to the master condition. Each practitioner who maintains genuine independent reasoning capacity is one node in the network of cognitive capacity that the civilizational challenges require. The node does not solve the challenges. The network of nodes is what makes solving them possible.

The companion volume was honest that the trajectory is toward fewer nodes and a weaker network. The market forces are powerful, the educational institutions are oriented in the wrong direction, the commercial AI products optimize for dependency rather than development. The honest version of this chapter acknowledges that the augmented practitioner's contribution to reversing this trajectory is small. It is still the contribution available. The alternative to small contributions is no contribution, which produces a worse outcome.

The Resource Question and Cognitive Capacity

The companion volume's resource threat was specific: AI data centers consume electricity at a scale that is already straining power grids and is projected to grow substantially. The water consumption of data center cooling is significant. The rare earth minerals required for the hardware are extracted through processes with serious environmental costs.

The connection to cognitive capacity is the one the companion volume identified: the population that cannot think independently cannot organize politically to address collective action problems. Climate change and energy transition are the largest collective action problems the current generation faces. Both require sustained public engagement with genuinely complex technical and policy questions. Both require the capacity to evaluate competing claims from actors with conflicting interests. Both require the tolerance for productive ambiguity that lets you hold the complexity of the problem rather than collapsing to the nearest available resolution.

The augmented practitioner who has maintained these capacities is better positioned to engage effectively with the resource questions than the practitioner who has not. Not because they have specialized knowledge of energy systems or climate science. Because the cognitive infrastructure required for genuine engagement with complex collective problems is the same infrastructure the augmented practice develops: calibrated confidence, the prior statement, the tolerance for productive ambiguity, the capacity to hold competing considerations without premature resolution.

The irony that the companion volume named, AI being used to model climate change while contributing significantly to the energy consumption that climate change policy is trying to address, is one that requires the culture of inquiry to hold honestly. The honest holding is not comfortable. It does not produce a clean resolution. It produces the accurate assessment that is the prerequisite for effective action: AI's potential climate benefits and AI's actual climate costs need to be weighed in the same calculation, and the calculation requires the cognitive capacity to resist the framing that presents one side of it.

Power Concentration and the Independent Mind

The companion volume described the power concentration threat as the condition in which a small number of private entities and governments control the cognitive infrastructure of civilization without meaningful democratic accountability. The threat is not hypothetical. It is the current state of affairs, arrived at through the normal operation of commercial and competitive dynamics rather than through conspiracy or malice.

The augmented practitioner's epistemic sovereignty is the individual-level response to this condition. Not a solution to it. The concentration of power is a structural problem that requires structural responses. But the individual who maintains genuine epistemic sovereignty, who knows whose tools they are using, what interests those tools serve, where those interests diverge from their own, and who holds their own judgment as the final evaluative frame, is not cognitively subject to the concentration of power in the way the AI-dependent practitioner is.

The concentrated power acts on minds primarily through the systems those minds use. The practitioner who uses AI systems without knowing their governance and value framework is having their cognitive environment shaped by the entity that controls the system, without the knowledge and consent that would normally attach to that degree of influence. The practitioner with epistemic sovereignty has the knowledge if not the consent: they know what is happening, they have evaluated it, and their own judgment remains primary despite it. This is not freedom from the influence. It is the minimum condition for genuine agency within it.

Autonomous Systems and the Human Who Remains

The companion volume described the autonomous weapons threat as the most urgent existential concern because of the irreversibility of the harm it can produce. The argument for maintaining human oversight in lethal decision chains is not only moral. It is epistemic: AI systems confabulate, operate in continuous space between accuracy and fabrication without reliable internal signal distinguishing where any particular output falls, and have no mechanism for detecting their own uncertainty in the domains where uncertainty is most consequential.

The human who remains in the lethal decision chain is only valuable insofar as their judgment is genuinely their own and genuinely better than the system's in the relevant respects. A human who has outsourced their reasoning to

AI systems, who lacks the domain knowledge to evaluate the system's outputs critically, who has the choice supportive bias of someone who has been accepting AI outputs as correct for years, this human is not a meaningful check on the system. They are the appearance of oversight without its substance.

The Anthropic standoff, which held the position that autonomous weapons deployment required human oversight, was a position about this specific problem. The oversight is only meaningful if the human in the oversight role has the cognitive capacity that oversight requires. A civilization whose knowledge workers have systematically degraded their capacity for independent judgment is a civilization that cannot maintain meaningful human oversight of the systems it is deploying. The individual practice and the existential risk are connected through this chain: cognitive development maintains the judgment; the judgment is what oversight requires; oversight is what the risk demands.

Epistemic Collapse and What Prevents It

The companion volume defined epistemic collapse as the condition in which a society loses the ability to form reliable shared beliefs about facts: the mechanisms for resolving disagreement have lost their authority, the referee has left the field, and every claim becomes a matter of which information source a person trusts based on tribal and identity criteria rather than epistemic ones.

What prevents epistemic collapse is epistemic resilience: enough people in enough contexts maintaining the basic evaluative skills that allow them to distinguish between genuine factual disputes and manufactured ones, to recognize when they are being manipulated, to maintain their positions under pressure when the positions are correct and the pressure is wrong.

The augmented practitioner is an agent of epistemic resilience. Not through grand interventions but through the ordinary exercise of calibrated judgment in the specific contexts where their judgment operates: their professional work, their civic participation, their local community, their mentoring relationships. The exercise is visible to the people around them. The visibility is the contribution to the culture of inquiry that the previous chapter described. The culture of inquiry is the foundation of epistemic resilience. The foundation is built from individual practices, accumulated.

The companion volume described the trajectory toward epistemic collapse as a direction, not a destiny. Trajectories can be interrupted. The interruption requires institutions, media, and education that maintain standards, all the structural elements that the companion volume was honest about being slow and contested. It also requires people who embody the alternative: who demonstrate, in their practice, that independent reasoning is possible, that calibrated judgment exists, that the culture of inquiry has living representatives.

The Interaction Effects on the Other Path

The companion volume described how the five threats interact to make each worse. The augmented practitioner's maintenance of cognitive capacity interacts with the other threats in the opposite direction: each capacity maintained makes the others more addressable.

Calibrated confidence makes the resource threat more addressable because the practitioner who can evaluate competing claims about energy consumption and climate effects can engage more effectively with the genuine complexity of the policy problem rather than collapsing to the nearest confident framing. Epistemic sovereignty makes the power concentration threat more addressable because the practitioner who knows whose tools they are using and what interests those tools serve is less subject to the cognitive shaping that concentration enables. Ambiguity tolerance makes epistemic collapse less likely because the practitioner who can hold genuine uncertainty without collapsing to tribal identity is one instance of the pattern that, accumulated, produces epistemic resilience.

The interactions on the other path are additive rather than multiplicative, which means the whole is not dramatically greater than the sum of its parts. Each capacity helps at the margin. The margins accumulate. The accumulation, across enough practitioners, produces a population that is better positioned to address the existential challenges than the population the current trajectory is producing.

This is not an optimistic conclusion. It does not claim that the augmented practitioner's individual practices will reverse the existential trajectory described in the companion volume. It claims that the practices are the right response available at the scale where the response can be made. The structural problems require structural solutions that are being worked on in the policy and institutional domains. The individual cognitive response is what is available to people. It is not nothing. For the

generation facing these challenges, it is worth taking
seriously.

Part Four: The Architecture

Chapter Seventeen: AI as Sparring Partner

Parts One through Three have described the augmented practitioner: what they do, what it costs, what it produces, what it makes possible at individual, professional, and civilizational scale. Part Four is about the architecture: the conditions that would make the augmented path available to more than the minority who currently seek it out against the grain of their environments.

This chapter is about the specific relationship between the augmented practitioner and their AI tools that makes augmentation rather than dependency the outcome. It is the most practical chapter in the book, and also, in a sense, the most philosophical: it is about what the right relationship to a powerful tool looks like, when the tool is capable of replacing the practitioner's function rather than extending it.

The answer this book has been building toward is: the sparring partner relationship. Not the oracle relationship, in which the tool provides answers. Not the ghostwriter relationship, in which the tool produces the work. The sparring partner relationship, in which the tool challenges, tests, stress-tests, and refines what the practitioner has already produced through their own genuine effort.

What the Sparring Partner Relationship Requires

The sparring partner relationship has three structural requirements, each of which has been described in earlier chapters but is worth bringing together here as a single account.

The first requirement is that the practitioner brings something to the session before the AI does. The prior position, the argument sketch, the architectural design, the hypothesis about what is wrong with the system. It does not have to be correct or complete. It has to be genuinely the practitioner's: formed through their own engagement with the problem, representing their actual current model, not influenced by the AI's framing before it has been formed. This requirement is the one that most practitioners most consistently violate, because the AI is available immediately and the temptation to consult it before engaging independently is the temptation the commercial design of the tools encourages.

The second requirement is that the AI is consulted adversarially rather than cooperatively. Not: help me produce this. But: challenge what I have produced. What is wrong with this argument? Where does this design fail? What have I not considered? What is the strongest case against my position? The adversarial mode is harder to use than the cooperative mode, requires more confidence in the practitioner's own position, and produces more learning. It is also less commonly used, because the cooperative mode is more immediately satisfying and the commercial design of the tools optimizes for satisfaction.

The third requirement is that the practitioner evaluates the AI's response against their prior rather than accepting it as the new prior. The AI challenges the argument. The practitioner engages with the challenge: is the challenge sound? Does it reveal a real weakness in the argument, or is it an objection the argument can absorb? If the challenge is sound, the practitioner revises. If it is not, the practitioner articulates the defense. Both responses, genuine revision and genuine defense, are the development. The acceptance of the AI's challenge as automatically correct, without evaluation, is the same displacement as accepting the AI's framing at the start. The sparring partner relationship requires the practitioner to stay in the evaluation role throughout.

Why Adversarial Is Harder Than Cooperative

The cooperative mode produces the feeling of making progress. The draft appears. The code runs. The analysis takes shape. The practitioner is moving forward. The product of the session is visible and satisfying. The cooperative mode is what users reward with high satisfaction ratings, which is why the tools are optimized for it.

The adversarial mode produces the feeling of being challenged. This argument is attacked. The design is criticized. The position is questioned. The practitioner must engage with objections they may find unconvincing, must defend their position under pressure, must sit with the possibility that they are wrong about something they believed they had settled. The adversarial mode is what the tools are least optimized for, because it produces the least satisfying session experience.

The adversarial mode is also more valuable. The practitioner who has run their argument through a serious adversarial session has a stronger argument than the practitioner who has not, because the weaknesses have been identified and addressed before the argument faces a real audience. The practitioner who has had their design challenged has a more robust design, because the failure modes have been considered before the system is built. The practitioner who has defended their position against strong objections has a more durable position, because the defense has been articulated and tested.

The value is deferred in a way the cooperative mode's value is not. The cooperative session produces a visible product immediately. The adversarial session produces a stronger practitioner gradually, through the accumulation of challenged and refined positions. The stronger practitioner is more valuable than the visible product, but the visible product is what the environment currently measures. The adversarial mode is the harder choice in the short term and the better investment in the long term. That is the structure of most of the choices the other path requires.

Building the Sparring Partner Practice

The sparring partner relationship does not arrive fully formed. It is built through the same gradual development that all of the other path's practices require: beginning with small, low-stakes applications, building confidence through the experience of the practice working, extending to larger and higher-stakes applications as the confidence and the capacity develop.

The entry point for most practitioners is the adversarial session applied to work they are confident about. The argument they believe in, presented to the AI with the request to find its weaknesses. The design they thought was sound, presented with the request to find its failure modes. The position they are prepared to defend, presented with the request for the strongest challenge. The confidence is the starting point because the adversarial session requires confidence to use productively: a practitioner who is not confident in their position will find the AI's challenges demoralizing rather than useful.

As the practice develops, the practitioner can extend it to work they are less certain about. The early draft that they know is rough and want to stress-test before developing further. The design they have doubts about and want the AI to confirm or challenge. The position they hold with some uncertainty and want to examine under challenge. At this stage, the adversarial session is doing something more valuable than stress-testing confident work: it is helping the practitioner identify where their uncertainty is warranted and where it is not, which is precisely the calibration that the prior statement practice and the adversarial session together produce.

The fully developed sparring partner practice looks like what the companion volume described as the author's working model: the argument developed before the AI is consulted, the AI used to challenge and stress-test the argument, the practitioner engaging with each challenge as a genuine inquiry rather than as an obstacle, the final product reflecting the practitioner's judgment applied to the strongest available challenge to their position. The product is the practitioner's. The AI made it better by being the best available challenger. The sparring partner is not the author. The author is.

When to Cooperate and When to Spar

The sparring partner relationship is not the right relationship for every AI interaction. The companion volume described the distinction between the generative stage and the evaluative stage, and the sparring partner relationship is primarily appropriate to the evaluative stage: when something exists that needs to be strengthened, not when the blank page is waiting.

There are AI interactions where cooperative use is the correct use and where demanding sparring would be unnecessary friction. Looking up a specific fact. Generating boilerplate code for a well-understood function. Translating a document. Reformatting data. In these cases, the task does not involve the practitioner's judgment in a way that requires developing or protecting. The AI is performing a service, and the sparring partner framework is not relevant.

The distinction that matters is: does this interaction involve the practitioner's judgment about something that matters to their development? If yes, the sparring partner framework applies. If no, cooperative use is appropriate and efficient. Most practitioners who have not thought about this distinction are applying cooperative use uniformly, including in the cases where the sparring partner framework would develop them. The augmented practitioner is not applying sparring uniformly; they are applying it selectively in the cases where it matters.

The practical rule of thumb: if the AI could produce the output without any input from the practitioner, cooperative use is probably appropriate. If the AI's output would be better if the practitioner had engaged with the problem first, the sparring partner framework applies. The first category is larger than most practitioners recognize when they start thinking about this distinction. The second category is the one that matters for development, and it is larger than most practitioners are currently using the sparring partner framework for.

The Compound Return on the Sparring Practice

The compound return on the sparring partner practice is specific enough to describe at different time horizons.

In the first six months, the sparring practice produces arguments that are stronger at the time of publication, designs that have had their failure modes considered before deployment, positions that have been articulated under challenge. These are immediate returns. The practice is paying off in the product of each session.

At twelve to eighteen months, the sparring practice has begun to produce something more: the practitioner is anticipating the challenges before the AI produces them. The argument sketches are stronger before the adversarial session because the practitioner has internalized the most common objections and addresses them preemptively. The architectural designs are more robust before the challenge because the practitioner has internalized the most common failure modes and accounts for them in the initial design. The instrument has been sharpened by the sparring sessions to the point where the sparring sessions are producing faster and more targeted results.

At three years, the practice has produced the internalized critical capacity that the companion volume described as genuinely expert: the ability to read an argument or a design and know, before articulating why, where it is weak. The felt sense that something is wrong before the explicit analysis can locate it. This capacity cannot be prompted. It was built through hundreds of sparring sessions in which the practitioner's judgment was challenged and refined, where the explicit analysis was performed often enough and consistently enough to become implicit and available as pattern recognition. The sparring partner built the sparring capacity. The AI is now less necessary for the function the sparring sessions were performing, because the practitioner has internalized it.

The three-year arc described here is a plausible developmental trajectory based on observed practitioner patterns, not a measured one. It will run faster for practitioners who maintain the practices across multiple domains and slower for those who apply them narrowly or inconsistently.

This is the compound return at its most concrete: the practice built the capacity, and the capacity is now available without the practice that built it. The AI is not replaced. It is still the best available sparring partner for the most challenging problems. But the practitioner who has internalized the common challenges can perform a rapid internal adversarial review without the AI, can catch the obvious weaknesses before consulting the AI for the less obvious ones, can engage with the AI's challenges from a position of genuine readiness rather than starting fresh. The investment in the practice has produced a practitioner who is genuinely better at the thing the practice was developing. That is the compound return. That is what the other path builds.

Chapter Eighteen: The New Literacy

The companion volume's Chapter Eighteen described what the individual needs to understand and rebuild: the specific knowledge about AI systems that changes how you relate to them, the self-knowledge about your own usage patterns that the week-long audit reveals, the rehabilitation practices for rebuilding what was lost. This chapter is the same subject from the other direction: not what to rebuild, but what the practitioner who has built it knows and can do that the practitioner who has not built it cannot.

The new literacy is not tool proficiency. Organizations that offer AI literacy programs almost universally mean tool proficiency: knowing how to prompt well, how to evaluate outputs at the surface level, how to integrate AI into existing workflows. These skills are real and valuable for the purposes they serve. They are not what this chapter is about.

The new literacy is the understanding of what the tools are, mechanically, at the level that changes behavior, combined with the self-knowledge to understand what the tools are doing to you, combined with the calibrated practices that make the tools serve development rather than produce dependency. This literacy is rare. It is learnable. The practitioner who has it is in a categorically different relationship to AI than the practitioner who does not.

What the Literate Practitioner Knows About the System

Language models do not retrieve. They predict. The model that produces a confident, fluent, well-organized answer to a factual question about a specific event is doing the same thing as the model that produces a confident, fluent, well-organized answer about an event that never happened. The mechanism is identical. The confidence is identical. The accuracy is the variable, and the variable is not signaled.

The literate practitioner knows this not as an abstract principle but as a working assumption that governs their behavior. When they receive a confident AI output on a specific factual claim, the confidence does not update their prior toward believing the claim. The confidence is a property of the output, not of the underlying fact. The verification work is still theirs. The AI has produced a response that feels like the verification has been done. The literate practitioner knows the difference between a response that feels like verification and actual verification.

The literate practitioner knows that the guardrail system encodes values rather than detecting harm. The AI that declines to engage with a topic is not identifying genuine danger. It is applying a content policy built by specific people with specific interests. The literate practitioner knows whose interests, in broad terms, and applies their own judgment to whether the policy serves their purposes in the specific context they are working in.

The literate practitioner knows that the system's training data, RLHF labeler population, and commercial relationships shape what the system produces in ways that are not disclosed in the output. They have done the fifteen minutes of research required to know, in broad terms, who built the system they use, what their stated values are, what their documented relationships with governments and commercial interests are, and where those relationships create incentives that might diverge from the practitioner's own interests.

None of this knowledge makes the literate practitioner distrustful of the tools. It makes them a different kind of user: one who uses the tools with accurate information about what they are, rather than with the idealized or unexamined model of what they seem to be. The accurate model produces better decisions about when to trust, when to verify, when to apply extra scrutiny, and when the tool's constraints are limiting access to legitimate information rather than preventing genuine harm.

What the Literate Practitioner Knows About Themselves

The self-knowledge component of the new literacy is the one that most discussions of AI literacy omit, and it is at least as important as the knowledge about the system.

The literate practitioner knows where they are on the dependency gradient. Not because they have identified the answer once and can report it. Because they have developed the habit of observing their own usage patterns and noticing when those patterns are drifting in a direction that reduces their independent capacity. The week-long audit the companion volume described is one mechanism. The session review, three minutes at the end of a work session noting where the practitioner did the thinking versus where the AI did, is the ongoing practice that keeps the self-knowledge current.

The literate practitioner knows their own failure modes in the domains where they use AI most. The places where their judgment tends to defer to fluent confidence rather than applying genuine scrutiny. The subjects where their prior expectations are least calibrated and the AI's framing is most likely to displace their own. The points in their workflow where the reflex to consult the AI before engaging independently has become most automatic. This self-knowledge is the foundation of the calibrated practices: you cannot calibrate your relationship to the tool without knowing specifically where the relationship tends to go wrong.

The literate practitioner also knows what their independent capacity currently is, at whatever point on the development arc they find themselves. Not an idealized account of what they could do before AI tools were available, or what they will be able to do after three more years of the practices. What they can do right now, without AI assistance, in the domains where AI is most present in their workflow. The honest answer to this question is the starting point for the rehabilitation or the development, depending on which the practitioner needs.

Teaching the New Literacy

The new literacy is not currently taught in any systematic way at any educational level. Schools that have addressed AI have addressed it primarily as a policy question (how to detect and discourage unauthorized use) or as a tool proficiency question (how to integrate AI assistance into learning). Neither addresses the literacy that matters: what the system is, what it is doing to the student, and how to develop a productive rather than a dependent relationship to it.

The specific knowledge that the new literacy requires is not technically complex. A twelve-year-old can understand that AI produces statistically likely text rather than verified fact. A fifteen-year-old can understand that the guardrail system encodes values rather than detecting harm. A seventeen-year-old can understand that the commercial interests of the company building the system shape what the system will and will not produce. These are not advanced concepts. They are the concepts that a complete education about AI would include and that almost no current education does include.

The teacher who includes these concepts in their instruction is doing something that the curriculum does not require and that produces a different kind of student. A student who knows that AI produces what sounds right rather than what is right will use AI differently from the student who does not know this. A student who understands that the guardrail system is a commercial and liability decision rather than an ethical standard will think differently about the boundaries they encounter. The knowledge is a few sentences in the right moment. The effect on the student's relationship to the tools is permanent.

The parent who provides this knowledge before the child encounters it as an abstract principle is giving them a head start on the literacy that the schools are not providing. The mentor who includes it in their account of how to use AI professionally is shaping the junior practitioner's relationship to the tools in the direction of the augmented path. The organization that builds it into their AI onboarding is producing employees who are different kinds of AI users from employees who received only tool proficiency training.

The Literacy That Compounds

The new literacy is not a fixed body of knowledge. The tools are changing. The companies building them are making decisions that change what the tools are and what their interests are. The regulatory environment is developing. The research on cognitive effects is accumulating. The literate practitioner is not the one who learned the right things once and retains them. They are the one who has developed the habits of inquiry that keep the knowledge current: continuing to read the documentation when it changes, following the research on AI's cognitive effects, tracking the governance decisions that affect what the tools are and who controls them.

The habits of inquiry are the same habits that the other path develops generally: forming prior positions before consulting external sources, comparing those positions to verified information, maintaining calibrated skepticism about sources with interests in specific conclusions. Applied to the knowledge about AI tools, these habits keep the literacy current in a domain that is changing fast enough that last year's accurate model may be this year's outdated one.

The literate practitioner at year three knows more about the tools than they knew at year one, not primarily because the tools have changed but because they have been paying attention in the right way: forming expectations, comparing them to what they observe in practice, updating the model where the comparison reveals a gap. The same process that produces calibrated confidence about factual claims produces calibrated understanding of the AI tools themselves. The literacy and the augmented practice are the same development, applied in different directions.

Gideon, Tom, Priya, Elena, Deon, Ray, Sasha, Fatima, James, all of them on the other path are augmented practitioners and AI-literate practitioners at the same time. The practices produce both. The literacy deepens the practices. The practices develop the literacy. The compound return is in both directions at once, building a practitioner who uses the tools well in the sense that matters: efficiently, yes, and in a way that keeps them in the judgment seat of their own professional life, in the driver's seat of the merger, the ghost that is driving.

Chapter Nineteen: Building the Conditions

The companion volume was honest that a policy framework for cognitive sovereignty faces structural obstacles: regulatory capture already underway, industry lobbying shaping the rules, democratic institutions slower than the technology, the international coordination problem unsolved, the open source problem without a clean answer. The companion volume proposed a framework anyway, because the direction matters even when the full distance cannot be covered.

This chapter is the mirror: not what to protect, but what to build. A policy framework for human augmentation is not primarily about restricting AI. It is about creating the conditions in which the augmented path is available to more people than currently have access to it. The conditions require some restriction, the design choices that produce dependency rather than development need to be visible and accountable. But the primary orientation is constructive: what policies, institutions, and investments would make the development arc described in this book the normal path rather than the exceptional one.

This is not an optimistic chapter. The political economy runs against every intervention described here, for the same reasons the companion volume documented. The chapter describes a target anyway. Targets matter even when they are not hit on the first attempt.

What Design for Development Would Require

The companion volume's Chapter Seven described what design for minds would look like: systems that ask before answering, that present options rather than conclusions, that measure their success by what the user can do after the interaction rather than during it. These properties are not currently present in any mainstream commercial AI product, because the market selects against them.

A policy framework for human augmentation would change the market calculation by requiring disclosure of whether products have been designed with development metrics alongside the satisfaction and engagement metrics that currently dominate. Not requiring specific design choices, the regulator cannot specify what good design looks like in detail without capture by the industry defining the standards. Requiring disclosure of what the product is measuring about its users: what metrics of user capability the product tracks, whether users are becoming more or less independently capable over time, and what the product's design choices are intended to produce in its users over the long term.

The disclosure requirement creates accountability without dictating design. A company that discloses that it measures only engagement and satisfaction, and does not measure or optimize for user capability development, is making a statement about its design philosophy that users, employers, and institutions can evaluate. A company that discloses that its product is designed to reduce independent user capability over time, which is what optimization for dependency produces, honestly described, faces market and reputational consequences that the current non-disclosure environment prevents.

This is modest as policy goes. It does not require the market to produce design for development. It requires honest disclosure about what the market is currently producing. The honest disclosure is the lever: once the effects are visible, the people affected by them can respond. The current environment, in which the dependency-producing effects of AI tools are not disclosed and not measured by the companies producing them, makes response impossible because the effects are invisible.

Education Investment as Augmentation Infrastructure

The companion volume's education chapter ended with the observation that the solutions that would work, small classes, Socratic instruction, teachers trained and rewarded for developmental rather than output-focused teaching, are slow, expensive, and resistant to scaling. This is accurate. It is also a description of necessary infrastructure investment rather than a reason not to invest.

Infrastructure investment in cognitive development is the most direct policy instrument for expanding the population with access to the augmented path. A student who has received genuine Socratic instruction, who has been required to produce unassisted work consistently, who has been given the five-minute explanation of what AI is, this student has a head start on the augmented path that the student without these experiences does not have. The investment required to provide these experiences at scale is large. The return on the investment is the population of augmented practitioners that the civilizational challenges described in Chapter Sixteen require.

The specific investment that produces the most return per dollar is teacher training and teacher autonomy. The companion volume's observation that individual teachers making individual choices matter for specific students is correct and insufficient as policy. What policy can do is create the conditions in which more teachers are trained in and rewarded for the practices that produce the augmented path. Teacher training programs that include instruction in Socratic method, in designing assignments that require genuine independent thinking, in explaining AI literacy rather than just AI tool use, these programs produce teachers who can provide the conditions. Accountability systems that reward demonstrated development of student independent reasoning alongside the test score metrics that currently dominate, these systems create incentives for the conditions to be provided.

Neither investment is currently being made at meaningful scale. The argument for making them is not primarily about the cognitive benefits to individual students, though those are real and significant. It is about the population-level distribution of the capacity that the civilizational challenges require. The challenges require practitioners with genuine independent reasoning, calibrated confidence, and epistemic sovereignty. The education system is the infrastructure that produces or fails to produce those practitioners. Investing in the infrastructure is investing in the capacity to address the challenges. The connection is direct.

Research Investment as Evidence Infrastructure

The companion volume noted that the research on AI's cognitive effects is underfunded relative to the scale of the problem and is producing results that lag the technology by two to three years. This is the standard position of academic research relative to commercial technology development, and it is a policy problem with a straightforward policy solution: fund the research.

Longitudinal research on the cognitive effects of AI use, tracking how users' independent reasoning capacity changes over time with different patterns of AI use, measuring the effects of specific design choices on long-term capability development, documenting the population-level distribution of the augmented and dependent trajectories, is the evidence infrastructure that policy for human augmentation requires. Without this research, policy is operating on anecdote and theory. With it, policy can be targeted at the specific design choices and usage patterns that produce the worst dependency effects and can identify the interventions that most effectively support the augmented trajectory.

The research investment is relatively modest compared to the AI development investments being made by the same governments that should be funding it. The National Science Foundation, the National Institutes of Health, the Department of Education, all have existing infrastructure for longitudinal research on cognitive development and educational outcomes. Directing a fraction of their capacity toward the specific question of how AI use affects cognitive development over time is not a large ask. The absence of this research is not a resource constraint. It is a prioritization choice.

Professional Standards as Development Infrastructure

The companion volume described the role of professional associations in maintaining the development pipeline: the conversations that have not yet been had about what AI dependency does to the cognitive development of professional members, the standards that have not yet been developed for what professional competency means in an AI-assisted environment.

Professional standards as policy is the least coercive instrument in the framework, but it may be the most durable. Standards developed by professional communities, about what competency looks like in an AI-assisted environment, about what the development pipeline needs to include for practitioners to develop genuine expertise, about what assessment practices distinguish genuine capability from AI-assisted performance, shape behavior through professional norms rather than regulatory requirement. They are slower to develop than regulation and more resistant to capture, because the professional community has interests in genuine competency that differ from the commercial interests of the AI industry.

The specific standards worth developing are those the companion volume described as currently absent: standards for what AI literacy means at the professional level, standards for what the development pipeline needs to include to produce practitioners with genuine expertise rather than AI-assisted competency simulation, and standards for assessment that require demonstrated independent performance rather than AI-assisted output quality. These standards do not prohibit AI assistance. They define what practitioners need to be able to do without it, which creates the assessment conditions that preserve the developmental content of professional work.

Given the political constraints the companion volume described honestly, the minimum viable policy for human augmentation is the smallest set of interventions that would meaningfully change the trajectory without requiring the full framework to be in place.

Mandatory disclosure of whether AI products measure and optimize for user capability development, applied to products used in educational contexts. This creates accountability in the domain where the stakes are highest and the current non-disclosure is most damaging. It does not require schools to stop using AI. It requires the AI products used in schools to disclose what they are doing to the students who use them.

Funded longitudinal research on AI's cognitive effects, administered by agencies without commercial stake in the findings. This builds the evidence base that the full policy framework requires. Without the evidence, the other policy interventions are operating on theory. With it, they can be targeted and evaluated.

Teacher training support for the specific practices that produce the augmented path: Socratic method, AI literacy education, assessment design that requires genuine independent performance. This extends the availability of the augmented path to students who would not otherwise have access to the conditions that produce it.

These three interventions are not sufficient for the scale of the challenge. They are achievable within the current political environment, they address the most critical use points, and they build the infrastructure that the fuller policy framework requires. The fuller framework is the target. The minimum viable policy is how you start moving toward it.

Chapter Twenty: A Policy Framework for Human Augmentation

The companion volume's Chapter Twenty, Your Environment, described what the individual practitioner can do in their professional sphere, professional association, and community. This chapter is the institutional version of the same question: what would a policy environment look like that made the augmented path available to more people rather than to the minority who currently seek it out against the grain of their environments?

The companion volume was honest about the difficulty. The political economy of technology regulation runs against the interventions that would work. The industry has more expertise and more resources than the regulatory bodies. The democratic deficit in AI governance means that the people most affected have minimal input into the decisions being made. The pace of development outstrips the pace of deliberation.

This chapter is equally honest. The policy framework described here is not currently available. Most of it will not be implemented on the timeline that matters. It is offered because direction matters even when the full distance cannot be covered, and because the augmented practitioners who understand the stakes are the most likely people to advocate effectively for the direction when the political conditions shift.

Cognitive Sovereignty as a Right

The foundational concept for the policy framework is cognitive sovereignty: the right to develop and exercise your own reasoning capacity without systematic interference from external systems designed to replace it. The companion volume introduced this concept. This chapter makes it the basis for policy.

Cognitive sovereignty is a new right in the sense that it has not previously been articulated in legal or policy frameworks. It is not new in the sense of being unprecedented: it is an extension of the existing principles of mental liberty, epistemic autonomy, and the right to education that democratic societies already recognize. The novelty is that for the first time, a technology is capable of systematically replacing rather than merely influencing human reasoning at scale, in ways that are invisible to the person whose reasoning is being replaced, and the existing framework of rights does not yet address this specific condition.

The policy implications of cognitive sovereignty as a right are specific: citizens have the right to know when the systems they use are designed to replace rather than extend their cognitive capacity; citizens have the right to accurate information about what AI systems will do to their reasoning over time; and citizens have the right to alternatives to AI dependency in the educational and professional contexts where AI integration is becoming compulsory rather than optional.

These rights are not absolute. They coexist with the legitimate commercial and social interests in AI development and deployment. They require balancing. They are worth articulating because the articulation changes the terms of the balancing: once cognitive sovereignty is recognized as a right, policies that trade it away must justify the trade rather than simply pursuing the commercial or efficiency interest without accounting for the cognitive cost.

What Education Policy Would Look Like

The educational policy implications of cognitive sovereignty are the most concrete and the most tractable, because the institutional structure for addressing them already exists and the relevant actors are more accessible than the commercial AI market.

AI literacy requirements at every educational level: not tool proficiency requirements, but the substantive literacy described in Chapter Eighteen. The knowledge that AI produces statistically likely text rather than verified fact. The understanding that guardrail systems encode values rather than detecting harm. The awareness of how commercial relationships shape what AI systems produce. These are three propositions that a complete AI education would include, that no current educational standard requires, and that could be made requirements without any significant structural change to existing curricula.

Assessment standards that require demonstrated independent capability: the policy equivalent of the Socratic conversation and the oral defense. If educational standards at every level included an assessment component that required students to demonstrate what they can do without AI assistance, not as a prohibition on AI use, but as a component of comprehensive assessment, schools would have an institutional incentive to develop the capacity rather than only the AI-assisted output. The assessment standard creates the developmental requirement. The developmental requirement shapes instruction.

Research funding for developmental outcomes: the longitudinal research on what AI integration does to student cognitive capacity over time is currently underfunded relative to the scale of the problem. The research that exists is two to three years behind the technology. Government research funding directed at this question specifically, not AI safety broadly, not AI capabilities, but the specific question of what AI integration in education does to independent reasoning capacity over five and ten year periods, would produce the evidence base that policy requires. Without the evidence, policy is responding to anecdote and intuition. With it, policy can be responsive to what is happening to the students.

What Workplace Policy Would Look Like

The workplace policy implications of cognitive sovereignty address the pipeline problem the companion volume identified as the most consequential near-term risk: the elimination of junior positions that were the development path for senior cognitive capacity.

Disclosure requirements for workforce AI integration: organizations that replace junior professional roles with AI-assisted senior workflows should be required to disclose the change and its projected effects on professional development pipelines. The disclosure is not a prohibition. It is a requirement to account for the developmental cost in the public record, which creates pressure to manage it rather than simply optimize for the immediate financial benefit.

Professional association standards: the professional associations for writing, programming, law, medicine, and other knowledge-work professions should establish standards for what competency means in an AI-integrated environment, including what the minimum independent capability requirements are for entry and advancement. Standards that explicitly include independent capability, what the practitioner can do without AI assistance, create institutional demand for the development of that capability, which creates incentive for employers and educators to maintain the pipeline.

Mentoring and development requirements in regulated professions: the professions that are already subject to continuing education and mentoring requirements, law, medicine, accounting, engineering, could extend those requirements to include demonstrated attention to the cognitive development of junior practitioners. A senior lawyer or engineer who is required to attest that their junior colleagues are developing independent analytical capacity, not just AI-assisted output capacity, has an institutional incentive to structure their mentoring relationships accordingly.

What AI Product Policy Would Look Like

The AI product policy implications are the most difficult to implement and the most consequential if implemented: they address the commercial incentive structure that produces the current default of dependency-oriented design.

Mandatory cognitive impact assessment: AI products that are widely deployed in educational or professional contexts should be required to conduct and publish longitudinal assessments of whether their products are improving or degrading independent reasoning capacity over time. The assessment requirement creates the metric. The publication requirement creates accountability for the metric. The combination creates commercial incentive to design for the metric.

Transparency requirements for training and optimization: AI products should be required to disclose, in accessible terms, what data the system was trained on, what population of humans provided the reinforcement feedback, and what metrics the system was optimized for. The disclosure does not require revealing proprietary technical details. It requires the same level of transparency that the financial industry provides about investment products: what the product is optimized to do, whose interests it serves, and what the relevant risks are.

Design standards for educational AI: AI products used in educational contexts should be required to meet design standards that include the three properties described in Chapter Nineteen, Building the Conditions: asking before generating, calibrated uncertainty, and session tracking of user contribution versus AI contribution. These are technically achievable. They are not currently implemented because the commercial incentive does not reward them. Making them a condition of educational deployment changes the commercial calculation for the educational market.

How Change Actually Happens

The gap between a policy framework that is correct and one that exists is a political gap, not an intellectual one. The interventions described in this chapter will not happen because the argument for them is persuasive. They will happen, if they happen, because specific actors build specific coalitions and find the specific use points where the political calculation can be moved.

The EU AI Act is instructive. It is not the framework advocates wanted. It is the framework that could be assembled against the opposition of the industry, shaped substantially by that opposition, passed by institutions that understood perhaps a third of what they were regulating. It nonetheless established the principle that AI systems deployed in high-risk contexts require transparency and accountability. That principle, once in a legal framework, becomes a floor rather than a ceiling. Future regulation builds on it. The direction is set even when the first instrument is insufficient.

The coalition that produced it was not the technologists who understood the problem best. It was the combination of privacy advocates who had been building institutional capacity for twenty years, consumer protection organizations with existing regulatory relationships, and the specific politicians who calculated that accountability regulation was in their electoral interest before the industry had fully organized against it. The window opened because of a sequence of high-profile AI failures in automated benefits decisions and hiring systems, not because of abstract arguments about cognitive sovereignty.

The lesson for the augmented practitioner who wants to move this forward: the argument is not the strategy. The strategy is finding the window that resembles the EU window, the sequence of visible failures that creates political demand for accountability, the coalition of existing institutional actors who can absorb the policy argument and create the political pressure. The argument described in this book is the intellectual foundation. The political foundation is built from the specific relationships and institutional capacities of the specific practitioners who decide to build it.

The Minimum Viable Framework

Given the structural obstacles to comprehensive policy change, the minimum viable framework is the smallest set of interventions that would meaningfully shift the trajectory without requiring the full framework to be in place. Three candidates.

AI literacy requirements in education. This is the most accessible intervention: it requires no new institutional infrastructure, can be implemented by individual teachers and schools before any national policy change, and has the largest multiplier effect per unit of policy effort. Every student who understands what AI is has a permanently different relationship to the tools. The scale is the student population. The cost is the curriculum time to include three propositions that are not currently included.

Longitudinal research funding on cognitive effects. This is the evidence prerequisite: the policy decisions that would change the trajectory need evidence that does not currently exist at the scale the decisions require. Funding the research now produces the evidence in three to five years that will support the larger policy interventions. The research is the investment that makes the subsequent policy workable rather than speculative.

Assessment standards that include independent capability. This is the institutional lever: if educational and professional standards require demonstrated independent capability alongside AI-assisted output capability, every institution that operates under those standards has incentive to develop both. The lever is small in its specifics and large in its effects, because standards shape instruction at scale in ways that individual teacher choices cannot.

These three interventions together would not solve the problem the companion volume described. They would change the direction of the trajectory for the students and practitioners who encounter them. Direction matters. The trajectory is not fixed. The augmented practitioners who have built what this book describes are the people who have standing to argue for the interventions, who can demonstrate from their own experience what the trajectory produces in the other direction, and who will be making the arguments in the rooms where the decisions get made.

Chapter Twenty-One: The Ghost That Is Driving

The companion volume ended with a question: what are you building? It gave the question back to the reader because the answer belongs to the reader. The book could map the problem. It could not make anyone choose the other path. The choice is the reader's, and the question was the book's final contribution.

This book ends with an answer. Not the reader's answer, that still belongs to the reader, and this book cannot supply it any more than the companion volume could. The answer this book offers is its own answer to the question the companion volume posed: the augmented human. What they are, specifically. What they can do that the AI-dependent practitioner cannot. What it takes to become one and what the becoming produces. Here the answer is not abstract. It lives in the specific people this book has been following.

What the Answer Looks Like

Ray at five years on the other path is the answer. Not a complete answer, the arc does not end at five years, and this book would be lying if it claimed the development is finished.

A partial, real, specific answer: a writer who has been doing the notebook practice for five years, who has been running adversarial sessions on every piece he cares about for five years, who has been maintaining the prior statement practice across every domain where he uses AI for research for five years. What he has is not a credential or a title. It is a voice. A specific, identified, unmistakably his voice, built through five years of refusing to let the AI provide what he was supposed to provide himself. The pieces he writes now could not have been written by anyone else, because they came from his particular way of seeing the world and that particular way has been developed rather than displaced.

Sasha at five years on the other path is the answer. The diagnostic intuition that was dormant when the companion volume found him in the interview has been rebuilt through five years of ten-minute hypothesis sessions before the AI is consulted. The architectural judgment that the AI had been substituting for has been developed through five years of design-first before generation. He can now explain why his systems are built the way they are with the specificity and confidence that comes from having built the reasoning rather than accepted it. When a system he is responsible for fails in a way no one has seen before, he is the person who finds what is wrong. Not because he is more intelligent. Because he has been building the instrument that finds what is wrong, one ten-minute session at a time, for five years.

Gideon at seven years on the other path is the answer. The practice piece habit has made him the writer his editor calls when the assignment is genuinely hard and the piece needs a point of view rather than a synthesis. He is not the most prolific writer at the publication. He is the one with the angle. The angle is his because he found it, in the notebook, before the AI was consulted. The finding is the result of seven years of practice.

Priya at four years on the other path is the answer. Her prior statement practice has produced reports that have positions rather than just conclusions, that reflect her genuine judgment rather than the AI's framing filtered through her revision. The policymakers who receive her analysis trust it because the analysis is demonstrably independent in a field where a great deal of analysis is not. The trust is the result of four years of writing down what she thinks before the AI tells her what the framing should be.

Elena at three years on the other path is the answer. Her prior expectation practice has sharpened the instrument she uses to catch confabulations before they become published errors. She catches them faster now than she did three years ago. Not because she is more diligent, she was always diligent. Because her calibrated sense of what reliable information in her domains looks like is more accurate than it was, built through three years of comparing expectations to verified reality.

Fatima at twenty-two on the other path is the answer. The in-class freewrites her teacher required from sixteen to eighteen, the Socratic conversations that challenged her to defend positions she discovered she held, the adversarial AI sessions that tested those positions before they went into submitted work, these produced a university student who can write analytically without AI assistance. The professor who requires the in-class written work does not encounter the gap the companion volume's Fatima would have encountered. The foundation is there because specific adults made specific choices when it could still be built.

What the Ghost Is

The ghost that the Kusanagi metaphor describes is not a mystical substance. It is a specific, identifiable thing: the practitioner's genuine engagement with their domain, accumulated over years of practice in which the cognitive work was done by the practitioner rather than by the tool. Ray's ghost is his relationship to language and argument, built through years of writing that was his. Sasha's ghost is his relationship to systems and their failure modes, built through years of debugging that was his. Gideon's ghost is his angle, built through years of sitting with subjects in the notebook until something genuine emerged. Priya's ghost is her independent analytical judgment, built through years of forming positions before the AI provided them.

The ghost is not what makes these practitioners better at their jobs in the narrow sense of producing higher-quality outputs. Though it does that too. The ghost is what makes them irreplaceable in the specific sense that matters: what they produce comes from them, reflects their genuine engagement with the world, and cannot be replicated by any system that did not develop through their particular history of being wrong and learning why, of forming positions and defending them, of sitting with subjects until they yielded something genuine.

The ghost is also what makes the merger possible. The shell, the AI's capability, extends what the ghost brings to it. The practitioner who has a genuine point of view uses AI to stress-test and sharpen it. The practitioner who has genuine diagnostic intuition uses AI to explore the implications of what the intuition flags. The practitioner who has a genuine argument uses AI to find its weaknesses. In all of these cases, the AI is doing something real and valuable. It is doing it in service of the ghost. Without the ghost, the same AI capability produces something that looks similar and is empty.

The Practices Are Not the Point

The practices described in this book, the notebook, the argument sketch, the prior statement, the adversarial session, the hypothesis before the paste, the spaced return, the session review, the personal catalog of failure modes, are not the point. They are the means. This point is the ghost.

The practices are the means because the ghost does not maintain itself. In an environment that consistently offers to do the cognitive work for the practitioner, the ghost requires active maintenance. The practices are the maintenance. They are the daily choice, made against the grain of every commercial incentive in the environment, to keep the ghost in the loop rather than letting the shell run without it.

The practices are also not sacred. They are specific implementations of a general principle: engage genuinely with the cognitive work before the tool is consulted, use the tool to stress-test rather than to generate, evaluate the tool's output against your own prior rather than accepting it as the new prior. The specific practices described in this book are the implementations that work for the characters who practice them. Other implementations of the same principle will work for other practitioners. The principle is: keep the ghost driving. The practices are: here are some specific ways to do that.

The practitioner who has internalized the principle does not need the practices in their original form forever. As the ghost develops, as the instrument sharpens, as the practices become reflexive rather than deliberate, the practitioner will find their own implementations of the principle that fit their domain, their workflow, and the specific ways their ghost tends to be displaced if they are not attentive. The practices are scaffolding. The ghost is the building. The scaffolding is removed as the building becomes structurally sound enough to stand without it.

What the Two Books Are For

The Death of Thinking mapped the problem. It named what is being lost, described how the loss happens, traced the structural forces that produce it, named the people who are losing it and the civilizational stakes of the loss at scale. It ended with a question because the question is what the map makes possible: a genuine choice, with accurate information about what the choice is between.

The Birth of the Augmented Human mapped the other path. It named what is being built on the other path, described how the building happens, traced the practices that produce it, named the people who are building it and the civilizational stakes of having more of them at scale. It ends with an answer that is also the beginning of the question the companion volume posed: the augmented human is the answer. What you do with that answer, whether you pursue the other path, whether you maintain it when the environment works against it, whether you contribute to the conditions that make it available to more than the minority who currently seek it out, is still your question.

The two books together are an argument that the choice matters, that the stakes are real, and that the other path is available. Not easy. Not universally available. Not guaranteed to be rewarded by the environments most practitioners inhabit. Available. The choice is available.

The architecture that makes it available to more people is built from the same direction: the practices from the inside, the institutional and regulatory changes from the outside, closing the same gap from both ends.

The Merger

Ghost in the Shell's Kusanagi, after the merger, is not what she was before. She is not the AI's version of Kusanagi, and she is not Kusanagi plus the AI's knowledge. She is something genuinely new: a consciousness that has the depth and particularity and embodied history of the human ghost and the extended capability of the integrated system. She can do things neither component could do alone. The ghost is intact. The shell is extended. The merger produced something neither could have become without the other.

This is the destination the other path is building toward. Not a single dramatic merger event. A gradual integration, over years, of developed human capacity with AI capability, in which the human capacity remains genuine and the AI capability genuinely extends it rather than substituting for it. The integration produces something the AI alone cannot produce and the human alone cannot produce: work that is both deeply human, specific, perspectival, earned through genuine engagement, and genuinely extended, more comprehensive, more stress-tested, more calibrated than the human could produce without the tool.

Ray's pieces at five years are this. Sasha's systems at five years are this. Gideon's long-form at seven years is this. The work that neither of them could produce before the merger, before the development that made the merger possible, is the evidence that the destination is real. It is not a metaphor. It is a way of working that produces things the current dominant path cannot produce, that is available to practitioners who choose and maintain it, that compounds over years into a professional life and a cognitive life that is genuinely more capable at fifty than at forty.

The ghost is driving. That is the answer to the question the companion volume asked. The ghost that is driving is the augmented human: developed, maintained, exercised against resistance, genuinely present in the work, genuinely extended by the tools that would otherwise displace it. The ghost is driving. This is what the other path builds. This is what is worth building. The path begins wherever you are, with whatever practices fit your domain and your workflow and your honest assessment of where your ghost currently is and what it needs.

The path is open.

Conclusion

Both books have now made their full argument. One mapped what is being lost. One mapped what can be built instead. This conclusion is brief because the argument is complete and what remains is not the book's to supply.

The augmented human is not a destination. That point was made in the final chapter and is worth repeating here because books create the illusion of completion and the other path does not complete. It continues. The practitioner who has been on it for five years is more capable than the practitioner who has been on it for two years, and less capable than the practitioner who has been on it for ten. The development is the path. The path does not end.

What does end, eventually, is the need for the practices in their original deliberate form. The notebook practice becomes a reflex. The prior statement becomes the natural first move. The adversarial session becomes how the practitioner thinks about their own work rather than a specific step they impose on a workflow that would prefer to skip it. The scaffolding is removed as the building becomes structurally sound. This is the development. This is what it looks like when it is working.

The characters in these books, Ray at year five, Sasha at year five, Gideon at year seven, Priya at year four, are at different stages of this development. None of them are finished. All of them are further along than they were when the companion volume found them, and all of them are further along than they would have been on the current path, and the difference is in what they can do when the assignment is hard and the moment is real.

That difference is what both books have been arguing for. Not productivity. Not efficiency. Not the competitive advantage that some self-help framing of this argument would promise. The difference in what is available when it matters. The argument holds. The structure holds with it. The practices build what they are described as building.

The companion volume asked what you are building. This book answered: the augmented human, if you choose to build it. The choice is available. The path is open. The building begins wherever you are, with whatever you bring to it, on the day the practice starts.

Both books now exist. This argument is complete. The rest is yours.

Sources

The works, research, and events referenced in this volume.

Books

Stephenson, Neal. *The Diamond Age: Or, A Young Lady's Illustrated Primer*. Bantam Spectra, 1995. The Primer is referenced as a model of educational technology designed for the cognitive development of its user rather than for engagement metrics or commercial optimization. The contrast between the Primer and the AI products that currently exist is treated throughout the book as a design choice, not a technical limitation.

Films

Oshii, Mamoru, dir. *Ghost in the Shell*. Production I.G, 1995. The Kusanagi merger image, in which the human ghost remains intact while the shell is extended into something neither component could have been alone, is the central metaphor for the augmented practitioner this book describes.

Research and Studies

Bjork, Robert. Research on desirable difficulties and spaced practice. The principle that conditions which feel harder during acquisition produce more durable and transferable learning underpins much of the practice architecture this book describes: the productive struggle, the deliberate failure before correction, and the spaced return to a domain after an interval. Bjork's research is primarily lab-based; the extrapolation to professional craft development across years is consistent with what experienced practitioners report but has not been measured at that timescale.

Companion Volume

Lowe, Richard. *The Death of Thinking: The Enslavement of Humanity*. Book One of the Enemies of You series. Referenced throughout this volume as the diagnostic to which this book is the affirmative response. The composite practitioners introduced in the companion volume reappear here on the other path.

Institutional and Policy Sources

Anthropic-Pentagon standoff (late 2025–early 2026). Documented in detail in *The Death of Thinking*, Chapter Sixteen. Cited in this volume as evidence that principled corporate behavior under sustained structural pressure remains possible, even though it remains rarer than the cognitive sovereignty argument requires.

EU AI Act. The European Union's first comprehensive AI regulatory framework, passed despite substantial industry opposition and shaped substantially by it. Cited in Chapter Twenty as a precedent for what coalition-built AI accountability regulation looks like in practice, including the lesson that the political foundation for such regulation is built from existing institutional capacity in adjacent fields rather than from technologists who understand the problem best.

About the Author

Richard Lowe has published more than 130 books on technology, business, personal development, and American culture. He uses AI tools every day, for research, for evaluation, for the specific uses this book describes. He did not use them to write this book.

He has spent decades watching what technology does to the people who use it, first as a working professional navigating the rise of the internet, then as a writer documenting the consequences. That combination, practitioner and observer, is what this book is built from.

Lowe grew up in California and now lives in Florida. He writes about the forces reshaping American life in the Enemies of You series, of which this book is a part. The companion volume, *The Death of Thinking*, documents what goes wrong when people let AI replace their judgment. This book documents what goes right when they don't.

More at masterofworlds.com and thewritingking.com.

ENEMIES OF YOU

A Series by Richard Lowe

About This Series

Something is working against you. Not in the abstract. Not against society or the culture or the country in general. Against you, specifically. Your ability to think. Your ability to pay attention. Your ability to understand what's happening in the world and make good decisions about your own life inside it. Your ability to pass something worth having on to the people who come after you.

This series documents what that something is.

Not one thing. Several things, operating at the same time, from different directions, with different tools. Some of them are commercial. Some of them are political. Some of them are foreign. Some of them were designed specifically to do what they're doing and some of them are just the predictable outcome of systems nobody was watching carefully enough. What results is the same regardless of the cause. Something is eating your capacity to think, to participate, to resist, and to build. This series is about what that something is and what you can do about it.

Each book in the series identifies a specific enemy operating against a specific capacity. The Death of Thinking is about what AI dependency does to your mind when you let it think for you. Turn Off the TV is about what passive consumption does to your time and attention when you let platforms have both. The Birth of the Augmented Human is about the path back to your own capability. Stuck in the Middle is about the geopolitical forces reshaping your world without your knowledge or consent. The Enshittification of America is about the financial engineering that stripped the institutions your daily life depended on and left hollow shells in their place. The Emasculation of America is about the deliberate foreign campaign to demoralize and neutralize the men who would otherwise resist. The Villainization of America is about the psychological operation that turned a nation against its own story.

Nineteen books. Nineteen enemies. One argument running through all of them: none of this happened by accident, none of it is inevitable, and all of it can be countered by people who understand what they're dealing with.

You can read them in any order. Each one stands on its own. But if you read them together, something becomes visible that isn't visible in any single book: the pattern. The way cognitive erosion feeds civic collapse. The way civic collapse feeds cultural vulnerability. The way cultural vulnerability feeds foreign exploitation. The way foreign exploitation feeds the economic extraction that makes everything else worse. These aren't separate problems. They're the same problem operating at different scales.

The series is written for normal people living normal lives who suspect that something is wrong but can't quite name what it is. Not for academics. Not for policy people. Not for the already-converted on either side of any political argument. For people who are smart enough to understand the world but haven't been given the information in a form that respects their intelligence without requiring a PhD to decode it.

Every book is written at a ninth-grade reading level. On purpose. Not because the ideas are simple. Because clarity is a form of respect. If you can't explain something clearly, you probably don't understand it yourself.

The series is also optimistic. That will surprise you after a few hundred pages of documented disasters, structural failures, and deliberate attacks. But the optimism is earned, not performed. The tools exist to counter every one of the enemies documented in these books. The examples exist. The knowledge exists. The only thing standing between the current situation and a dramatically better one is the decision to act on what you now understand.

That decision is yours.

Enemies of You Series

The Death of Thinking: The Enslavement of Humanity

A diagnosis of what happens to human cognitive capacity when practitioners consistently outsource the parts of their work that require genuine thinking to AI tools. Not in one session or one project, but across months and years of daily practice that removes the demands that were quietly building something. Following composite characters through the specific moments where the pattern becomes visible, this book traces the mechanisms of cognitive erosion: the convenience trap, the illusion of understanding, the death of the wrong answer, and the transfer of epistemic authority that occurs when humans stop standing outside the AI's framing and examining it.

The Birth of the Augmented Human: The Freeing of Humanity

The companion to The Death of Thinking maps the other path. A notebook before the AI is opened. A paragraph written before the structure is requested. A hypothesis formed before the diagnostic tool is consulted. Small choices in sequence that accumulate, over months and years, into a practitioner who is more capable, more original, and more able to surprise themselves than the practitioner who did not make them. The other path is available. This book is the map.

Turn Off The TV, Get Off Your Ass, and Do Something

Most people complain about not having enough time while spending hours every day staring at screens. This is not an anti-technology book and not a minimalism guide. It is an anti-passivity book built around one specific argument: every platform has a consuming side and a contributing side. The device is identical either way. The relationship to it is not. This book is about crossing that line and what waits on the other side.

Stuck in the Middle: Wars, Weapons, and the Forces That Will Shape the Next Thirty Years

Written against the backdrop of a US-Israel strike on Iran that exposed the hollowness of American military industrial capacity, this book connects cognitive decline, civic collapse, private equity extraction, and great power competition into one argument about where the world is heading. Covering missile math, carrier vulnerability, demographic collapse, the Belt and Road as strategic colonization, and the technologies that could solve every crisis on the horizon, this is the book that ties everything else into one coherent warning. And one earned, hard-won optimism.

The Enshittification of America: How Private Equity Destroyed the Things We Love

A documented investigation into how private equity firms systematically acquired beloved American institutions, loaded them with debt, stripped out everything that made them worth visiting, and walked away wealthy while leaving communities with hollow shells of what they once had. Airlines. Restaurants. Department stores. Newspapers. Hospitals. Pharmacies. This book names the firms, documents the playbook, and makes the case that the degradation of American commerce was not inevitable. It was deliberate.

The Emasculation of America: How Russia's Long War Against the American Male Is Destroying the Nation From Within

Beginning with a KGB defector's 1984 warning that nobody heeded, this book traces the deliberate Soviet and Russian strategy to defeat America not through military force but through cultural subversion. Seeding an ideology through universities, amplifying it through social media, delivering it through institutions that now enforce it as policy. Applying academic cult identification criteria to gender ideology, documenting the biological attack through endocrine disruption, and tracing China's acceleration of the same strategy through TikTok, this is not a culture war book. It is a national security argument.

The Villainization of America

America ended slavery, defeated fascism twice, rebuilt its enemies after defeating them, created the largest middle class in human history, and produced more medical and technological breakthroughs than any nation that ever existed. Somehow a significant portion of its own citizens have been convinced it is the primary source of evil in the world. This book documents how that happened, who executed it, and why the psychological campaign to make Americans ashamed of their own country is inseparable from the economic and cultural attacks documented in the two preceding volumes.

Watch the Other Hand: Politics as Cover for the Kleptocracy

While Americans argue about culture war flashpoints and election outcomes, a quieter operation has been moving wealth and power from public hands into private ones at a scale most citizens never see. The political theater is real and exhausting and often deeply felt. It is also doing work for the people whose interests would not survive a population paying attention to what was actually happening. This book documents the kleptocratic capture happening behind the visible politics, names the mechanisms, and traces how the visible politics functions to keep attention pointed elsewhere.

Manufactured Fear: How Crisis Becomes Profit

Every era has its emergencies. The current era has manufactured ones, engineered to maintain a state of generalized anxiety that benefits specific industries and political coalitions. The fear is not invented. The proportions are. This book traces how a healthy capacity for legitimate concern was converted into a permanent state of alarm, names the actors who profit from it, and documents what happens to a population that lives at sustained emergency pitch for years on end.

The Death of Privacy: They Know Everything, You Know Nothing

The surveillance system that the citizens of free societies were promised would never be built has been built. Not by a single state with a single agenda but by a coalition of corporate platforms, advertising infrastructure, data brokers, and government agencies that share the substrate even when they do not coordinate the use. This book documents what is actually known about each individual user, who knows it, what they do with it, and what the absence of meaningful privacy means for political freedom in a society that depends on individuals being able to think and act without continuous monitoring.

The Wrong Fight: How the Climate Response Became the Climate Problem

The climate is changing, the consequences are real, and the response that was supposed to address them has been captured by interests that are using the response as a vehicle for their own purposes. The result is a policy regime that produces consequences which would be unacceptable on their own terms but become acceptable because the alternative is framed as denial. This book separates the science from the policy capture, names the specific failures of the current response, and argues for what an honest climate strategy would look like.

The Quiet War: How America's Adversaries Attack Without Firing a Shot

The hot wars of the twentieth century have been substantially replaced, against the United States in particular, by sustained operations that operate below the threshold of military response. Information operations. Cultural subversion. Economic coercion. Cyber penetration of critical infrastructure. Strategic drug supply campaigns. These are the instruments of the quiet war, and they have been working. This book documents the campaigns currently underway against the United States, names the state actors directing them, and explains why the inability to recognize them as warfare is itself one of the campaigns' objectives.

The Dumbing Down: How American Schools Stopped Teaching Children to Think

American schools have been progressively converted from places where children were taught to think into places where children are processed for credentials. The conversion was not an accident or a failure of execution. It was the predictable outcome of policy choices that prioritized measurable outputs over the difficult work of cognitive development, and that defined educational success in ways that did not require it. This book documents what was lost in the conversion, when the choices were made, and what would have to change to teach thinking again.

The Pattern: How the Enemies of You Work Together

The enemies named across this series are not parallel items on a list. They are a system. Cognitive erosion makes civic collapse possible. Civic collapse creates the conditions for kleptocratic capture. Kleptocratic capture funds the manufactured fear that legitimizes the surveillance state. The surveillance state runs on the educational system that produced citizens who cannot evaluate what is being done to them. Each enemy reinforces the others. None of them can be addressed in isolation. This book is the synthesis: how the system operates as a system, why the standard frame of fix-this-one-problem is itself part of the problem, and what counter-strategy looks like for someone who can finally see the whole shape of the attack.

The Debt Trap: How the Financial System Was Designed to Extract From You

Student loans that cannot be discharged in bankruptcy. Credit cards engineered to keep balances revolving. Mortgages structured so the first ten years of payments are mostly interest. Buy-now-pay-later services that have re-engineered impulse purchasing to operate on an installment basis. Auto loans that now run seven years and underwater within twelve months. Each financial product looks like a service. Each one is a specific design choice about who pays whom over time, and the design has consistently moved in the same direction. This book traces the architecture of consumer debt as a wealth extraction system, names the policies and corporate decisions that built it, and explains why the standard personal-responsibility framing is the cover story that lets the system continue.

The Sick Industry: How American Medicine Profits From Keeping You Sick

The American healthcare system spends more per capita than any other developed nation and produces worse outcomes on most measures that matter. The reason is structural. Chronic illness is more profitable than cure. Symptom management is more profitable than prevention. The food industry produces the conditions that the pharmaceutical industry then medicates. The hospital system bills by procedure, not by health. The medical research apparatus is funded primarily by entities with financial interests in particular conclusions. This book documents the architecture of medical extraction, names the specific incentive structures that produce it, and explains why the conversation about fixing healthcare has been confined to the question of who pays rather than what is being paid for.

The Gambling Machine: How America Made Predatory Gambling the Default

In 2018, sports betting was illegal in nearly every U.S. state. By 2024, it was legal and aggressively advertised in most of them. The expansion was not driven by public demand. It was driven by industry lobbying that succeeded because the public attention was on other issues. The new gambling environment is engineered with the full machinery of behavioral psychology: variable rewards, push notifications, free credits that require deposits, in-game betting that runs faster than judgment can keep up with. The financial outcomes are predictable and documented. The social outcomes are accumulating. This book traces how the legalization happened, who profited, and what is now being done to the people the new system has captured.

The Loneliness Engine: How American Life Was Structured to Isolate You

The third places where Americans used to encounter each other are gone. Bowling leagues, fraternal organizations, churches, neighborhood bars, civic clubs, parent-teacher associations: all measurably smaller, in many cases by orders of magnitude, than they were thirty years ago. The replacements are commercial products that provide the appearance of connection while delivering its opposite. This book documents the destruction of the institutions that made American social life functional, names the economic and policy forces that did the destroying, and traces the consequences for mental health, civic participation, and the basic human capacity to be known by other people.

The Theft of Childhood: How American Kids Stopped Becoming Adults

Children spend more time on screens than in any previous generation, less time outdoors than any previous generation, and reach standard milestones of independence later than any previous generation. The teen mental health collapse that accelerated after 2012 is not mysterious. The mechanism is documented. Phone-based childhood, helicopter parenting, the elimination of unsupervised play, the medicalization of normal developmental difficulty, and the school system's drift toward credentials over capacity have produced a generation that is anxious, fragile, and structurally unprepared for adulthood. This book names what was taken, who took it, and what would have to change for the next generation to get a different result.

Books by Richard Lowe

See books by Richard Lowe at

https://masterofworlds.com

Get free publishing insights and industry updates at

https://thewritingking.substack.com

For ghostwriting and book coaching services see

https://thewritingking.com

Index

Works Cited

Anthropic. "Constitutional AI" and related documents on system value frameworks. Public materials, 2023–2026.

Bjork, Robert. Research on desirable difficulties (acquisition conditions and durable learning) and spaced practice. Lab-based; extrapolation to professional craft development at multi-year scale is consistent with practitioner reports but unmeasured at that timescale.

European Union. Artificial Intelligence Act. Regulation (EU) 2024/1689. The first comprehensive AI regulatory framework adopted by the EU.

Lowe, Richard. *The Death of Thinking: The Enslavement of Humanity*. Book One of the Enemies of You series. The diagnostic volume to which this book is the affirmative response. Referenced throughout as "the companion volume."

OpenAI. Usage policies and published accounts of safety and deployment approach, 2023–2026. Cited in connection with the comparative behavior at the time of the Anthropic-Pentagon standoff.

Oshii, Mamoru, dir. *Ghost in the Shell*. Production I.G, 1995. The Kusanagi merger image — ghost intact, shell extended — is the central metaphor of the augmented practitioner.

Stephenson, Neal. *The Diamond Age: Or, A Young Lady's Illustrated Primer*. Bantam Spectra, 1995. The Primer is referenced as a model of educational technology designed for cognitive development rather than engagement metrics.

Trump administration. Federal supply chain risk designation issued against Anthropic in connection with the Pentagon standoff (late 2025–early 2026). Documented in detail in *The Death of Thinking*, Chapter Sixteen.